Mission

Ready

Marriage

My Life as an Active Duty Wife

Claire Roberson Wood

Printed in the United States of America

First Printing, 2015
ISBN 978-1-63192-929-8

BookBaby Publishers

Cover Design: Claire Roberson Wood
Cover Image: Jennifer Woods Photography

This book is dedicated to all of the faithful military spouses who have served before me and to those who will serve long after.

Contents:

Foreword

There comes a time in the life of every person when she must evolve and go through a certain metamorphosis. This change is difficult and it requires time and often perspective. In my life I have had tremendous difficulty navigating these changes with grace. Therapists call them adjustment periods. I call them crises of faith.

In my own experience, I have had to navigate new waters (so far) in three such stages and major life events. For me, the first was *marriage*, next came *motherhood* and most recently was our family foray into life in the *military*. These events have been spaced out over more than a decade, giving me time to adapt over a period of years. For many military spouses the order can be different and for some, these major life events can come all at once. How we choose to react to these circumstances can determine our course for years to come. Who we lean on and how we cope can lead to a life of joy or a life of absolute misery. I want to choose joy!

Today's military spouse faces challenges and trials that are unique. With a landscape of global anti-terrorism, a waning lack of national patriotism and multiple deployments, dependents are having to maneuver difficult circumstances. Despite our near constant connectivity through technology and social media, many military spouses are feeling more isolated, alone and hopeless than ever before.

Soldiers aren't simply coming home from deployments and settling into life after a war's end. These days, our beloved soldiers and spouses are turning right around and being sent again. And again. And again. These dynamics affect the way military spouses relate to their marriages and military life in a way unlike those who have served before us.

With recent media attention on these stresses and pressures military spouses face, I am reminded of the dire need for a resource in the hands of dependents. Not only are military spouses, now, more than ever, in need of resources; they are most in need of hope! Our nation has been at war for over a decade. With this comes physical, mental and emotional demands and exhaustion on our service members, our marriages and our families.

If you have come to this book looking for guideposts or formulas for a happy, healthy marriage, you have come to the wrong place. You won't find a step by step plan for making your spouse a better partner, more sensitive to your needs or how to make him a more effective leader in the home. You won't find admonitions to pray together more, have more date nights or the secrets to better communication or intimacy. Having a mission ready marriage *does* require prayer, connection, intimacy and communication, yes. But that's not what this book is about.

There is power in sharing our stories and testimonies of how difficult trials can bring about good in our lives. This book is a story. It is *my* story. I share my own experiences with navigating a new life in the world of the military. I was wide-eyed, fearful, clueless and at several turns lacked the appropriate wisdom and faith to find my way.

I've been on a quest to seek a better understanding of this unique life while looking at it through the lens of my faith. I discovered that I don't need platitudes and trivial mottos. As military spouses, sometimes what we need to read or hear is that what we are experiencing is normal and that yes, we will get through it. This is my wish for this book. Hear my stories, share in my struggles, glean wisdom from my mistakes and find hope.

While I can't change my husband, the Army, tiring battle rhythms, or countless other factors out of my control, I have learned that the only one I *can* change is me. The only person I *can* fully rely on is God. If I want a dynamic marriage and partnership that is mission ready, I need to first examine myself. If I want to thrive as a military spouse, I need to hold up a mirror to my own actions and reactions.

As I have poured over dozens of books on the shelves of libraries and bookstores here is what I have been looking for: I have been looking for honesty. I have been searching (sometimes frantically) for a current, unsentimental glimpse into the *real* struggles of military life today.

We are a generation of military spouses who are long past the decorum and antiquated customs of being silent bystanders as dependents. We need more than slogans and campaigns to keep ourselves, our families, and our marriages strong. We need tools to help us navigate the course. We need hope through our faith in Christ; a hope that is bigger and greater than our nation and ourselves.

Introduction

My husband, Ryan and I are entering into our second decade of marriage. All the time, we are hearing about someone else we know whose marriage is over because of extra-marital affairs and broken promises. It is heart-breaking and I can't begin to fathom the pain that must follow when a marriage is dissolved, a family unit is forever changed, and a covenant is no longer being honored. And yet, I can see how it happens. Life is hard. Being married to another person, living with them, sharing in life's responsibilities, putting your needs behind someone else's does come with its challenges.

Being married is both rewarding and difficult at the same time. It is one of life's most cherished blessings to live alongside someone you love. It is also one of the aspects of life that takes constant work and attention if it is going to be successful. *Marriage is hard work* and many would argue that military marriages take even more effort to thrive.

Marriage takes constant work, attention, and nurturing. Major life events like the death of a loved one, moving/relocation, job changes, health problems, difficulties with children, or financial turmoil only add strains and stresses to the marriage relationship.

The pressures of life in the military magnify and multiply that fragility exponentially. According to an article in a 2013 volume of the <u>Clinical Child and Family Psychology Review,</u> *"data suggest(s) that overseas deployment, exposure to combat, experiencing or participating in violence during war deployment, service member injury or disability, and combat-related post-traumatic stress disorder (PTSD) all have profound impacts on the functioning of military families."*

Life in the military is demanding. It requires much and so often what it takes from us we never get back. Take any of the stressors from the data listed above and you have a recipe for a difficult marriage. Add in *more than one* or *all* of those components, and it really is a miracle that any military marriages survive at all. The question at hand is, *"How can our marriages function and flourish when they are indeed so fragile?"*

It is my desire to share some personal anecdotes from my own experience. I want to share some of my own insights into how I might have handled certain transitions differently if given the chance. In each chapter you'll find a section called *"<u>What I Needed</u>."* I try to give an open account of some practical steps I could have and *should* have taken when life and the Army handed me a difficult situation.

Each chapter also includes *"<u>What He Needed</u>"* where I try to see circumstances from the perspective of my husband. Although Ryan is a Christian, I aim to offer insights that could fit any man regardless of where he stands spiritually. Marriage is a two-for-one. There are two parties involved, but so often I am selfish and often only think of how life affects me. In this portion of each chapter I hope to broaden my view of how military life and my reaction to it could more positively affect my marriage in order to make us stronger and more mission ready.

I have included some excerpts in each chapter "*From My Blog*," which are personal reflections from my online journal. You will quickly see that I'm often a crybaby, super sensitive and overly emotional. I've tried to include passages in real time from when some of the Army's more demanding moments have held me captive.

As each chapter draws to a close, I have included a section called, "*God's Use for the Trial*." I am a firm believer that when we walk through difficult seasons, there is purpose behind it. I think there is wisdom in reflection and looking to see how God is present in our times of trouble and difficulty. He uses our circumstances to draw us into a closer relationship with and dependence upon Him. It is through Christ we can walk in hope.

Finally, the chapters each end with a series of five "*Questions for Reflection*." These questions are perfect for making the chapter personal to one's own experience. They can easily be used privately for journaling starters or for contemplative thought. Another way the questions could be used is for a small group discussion among a women's group or Bible study. The chapters are set up for use on a 13 or 14 week semester.

As military spouses *we* have a big assignment set out before us. We have the honor and duty of helping to support our spouses and their professional missions on the home front. More importantly, long after my husband's military service may end, it's my wish that my marriage and my faith in God would survive intact and be stronger than before.

I want a marriage that not only withstands the challenges of military life. I want a marriage that thrives and grows and stands strong until death-do-us-part. I want a mission ready marriage. In order for that to happen, I have to make my own heart mission ready first.

I pray that the Lord would continue to use the lessons He is teaching me through my own experiences to shed light on His faithfulness and goodness! I pray that my stories and the lessons I have learned along the way will help *you* to make *your marriage* mission ready as well.

Chapter 1

Life Before the Military: How in the World Did We Get Here?

I did not grow up in the military. My dad never served and only one of my grandfathers did a short stint in the U.S. Navy right out of high school. He never saw any war time. My dad's uncle, a man I saw only at Thanksgiving is literally the only person in my family of origin with any significant military associations. Uncle Carlos never spoke much at our family meals each November. I think the most I ever heard him say was *"Move out of the way so I can see the television."*

Simply put, the military has never been on my radar. I joke that my only serious observances of anything military related were getting days off from school on federal holidays. My gratitude for anyone serving at home or abroad was found in my ability to sleep in on a Monday instead of sitting in class. I have pledged allegiance and stood during the National Anthem, but this is where my understanding of the military ended until a few years ago.

Many of the wives I have met during these past few years after my husband went on active duty have a much different experience. Many have grown up Army Brats or Navy Brats (a term I still don't know how to translate). Many were married right out of high school or the minute their soldier finished Advanced Individual Training (AIT). Many wives have known more years as a dependent than they ever did in the civilian world.

Such is not the case for me. I grew up in the same town where my parents and grandparents grew up. I saw my grandparents, aunts, uncles, and cousins on a weekly basis. I went to elementary school, junior high, and high school with the same group of friends. Even when Ryan and I married in 2001, we were only living about half an hour away from our entire extended families.

Our three children were born in rapid succession in 2003, 2005, and 2007. Looking back, I don't know how we would have made it without the extra sets of hands and all of the support of our extended families. During those years, Ryan was a full-time seminary student and full-time youth pastor. Between pregnancies I worked part-time as an adjunct teacher at the university I attended. Life felt full and easy. We felt like we really had everything we needed. Our entire world could be found inside the bubble of a few surrounding zip codes.

It was during this time that we felt a divine stirring in our hearts. The plans we had laid out for ourselves and our intentions of eventually being in a full-time role as a senior pastor of a local church in our denomination, were shifting and changing. Life was good, yes. But we felt God getting ready to move us out of our comfort zone.

Through the course of almost two years of much prayer, counsel-seeking, and tearful discussions (on my part), we finally felt a specific plan forming for our future. In May of 2010, Ryan submitted a cache of paperwork and began a series of interviews both with our denominational Chaplain's Commission and the U.S. Army. By December of that same year, he had been picked up for an active duty slot for the May 2011 Chaplain Basic Officer Leaders Course (CH-BOLC) at Fort Jackson in Columbia, South Carolina.

We literally had no clue that we had just signed our lives away! Throughout the spring of 2011, our family finished up our tenure at the church where we were serving. I finished my last semester of college teaching. Our kids completed their school/pre-school year and spring sports. We packed up and moved out of our parsonage we had lived in for six years. Ryan kept out his personal belongings for a twelve week school, and our three children and I kept out a few things to go live with my parents during that transition time. The familiar life we had known for the past three decades was being boxed up and neatly arranged on a transportation truck headed to our first duty station.

There was some low level anxiety already brewing in me. I began to get nervous that maybe we'd made the wrong decision; maybe we'd heard God wrong. *"Lord, are You SURE You picked the right family for this adventure?"* I seriously began to doubt that our marriage would survive the twelve week separation. I knew my parenting limits would be tested as a solo parent for three months. I started to really sweat the big and small stuff. We had been living warmly and cozily in our nest with many warm and cozy nests of everyone near and dear to us all in the same tree. I wondered, *"Why did we think joining the Army was a good idea?"*

When Ryan left for CH-BOLC, it felt as if we purposely jumped right out of that nest into the free-fall of zero control over our future. It was as if we had said with a certain sense of gullibility, *"Here Army, we are yours...send us where you want. Our life is in your hands. You are at the helm, you make the decisions and call the shots. We will go where you send us."* And for me that felt like I had given up way too much control. It felt unnatural and honestly, it felt crazy.

Who in the world gives up their freedom and life, their wishes and choices about where to live and raise a family? In those early moments when we realized that we were really doing this thing, I had many doubts and fears. We had signed our lives away for at least a three year active duty commitment with an additional five year add on of Army Reserves or National Guard. There was no escape plan.

There was no backing out. It was time to fly or take a nose dive out of that nest right into the ground.

In hindsight, all of my worries about giving up control and not holding the reigns in our own life were absurd. You see, Ryan and I had already been living a life in submission to God long before the Army came into the picture.

Individually, we had each submitted our lives and bowed our knees to the Lordship of Jesus Christ as young people. As a couple, we had both submitted our lives as we knelt and took communion and said our vows at our wedding ceremony. And every year since, at the heart of our decision making was always a period of prayer and seeking the face of God as the master Author of our story. We had already begun our journey with Someone else calling the shots. God had called us and guided us at every step of our marriage, vocations, and ministry thus far. He was still doing it. We were just placing ourselves in His hands again, only this time, that submission took on the form of the United States Army.

What I Needed:

During this transition, what I needed was a sounding board. It was difficult to express many of my concerns and worries to our families. For starters, they didn't have much wisdom or expertise in the matters of military life either. Our families had no basis for knowing what we were in for. They kept us on our toes with questions for which we had no answers. As someone who wanted to feel like we had a firm grasp on and new confidence in our new future, it felt embarrassing to respond to their queries with *"We don't know."*

I also felt at odds sharing my fears about this venture because in all honesty, it was hard on our families seeing us say goodbye. It was painful for them to imagine their lives without us right around the corner to share in memory making, holidays, just-because drop-ins, or last minute dinner plans. Although it was never spoken out loud, the unspoken tension was *"If you are so upset or unsure about this undertaking, then why did you choose it?"* And that strain was difficult for me. I felt as if I couldn't vent, cry, or process my concerns because no one really understood why we were doing this. No one could grasp why we signed up for this life in the Army.

At this earliest of junctures in our military career, I had no network of other military spouses to glean encouragement from or with whom to find solidarity. Truly, other than our denominational endorser and his precious wife, Richard and Brenda, there was no one in my life I could get answers from about what we should expect. At the time, that friendship was new and so I felt out of line assaulting our endorsers with a million silly questions. Without a sounding board or some seasoned military spouses speaking their wisdom over me, I felt exceptionally alone and without proper resources to help me settle into what our new life was about to look like. I wanted a bulleted list or handbook that would spell out very clearly what being an Army spouse entailed.

During Ryan's final week of CH-BOLC, the families were invited to attend several days of activities. To say the week was traumatic for me is a gross understatement. I was like a volcano ready to erupt with all of the emotions I had been holding inside for months.

I was happy to see our children reunited with their daddy. I was overjoyed to have my partner back even if we were in temporary bachelors' quarters, still living out of our suitcases. At this point we were days away from making the trek to our first duty station. And the closer it got to pulling out and driving away from our old life the more fearful I became. The second guessing about what we had signed up for became nearly constant. I was exhausted from the weight of being a single parent, living in my parents' upstairs, and a summer of travel. I was anxious about the particulars of leaving South Carolina to set up a life in Texas two time zones away.

The graduation week festivities included a two day seminar set aside just for chaplain spouses. It was meant to be helpful and informative. It was meant to give a room full of over 100 wives access to some question and answer time. It was meant to give us a magnitude of information in matters such as how to navigate Tri-Care health insurance, proper etiquette at a ball or coffee, helpful tips on surviving a deployment, and encouragement to get involved in a chapel community on post.

I cried twice in those meetings over the course of two days; once when I excused myself from the room to talk myself down from an actual panic attack and once in front of a very gracious and understanding senior chaplain's wife, Karen, who offered me a hug.

This week was the first I was hearing about the effects of a deployment on a marriage and on children. It was the first time I was really letting it sink in that the Army came first. It was the first time I realized that my kids would need a strong male role model like a neighbor or uncle while their daddy was away at war. It was the first time I was hearing about the casualty notification process. It was the first time I was hearing how I would need to rely on other spouses in the form of auxiliary ministries, Family Readiness Groups

(FRGs) and spouse coffees. It was the first time I heard about what a Care Team is. I felt absolutely positive that I did NOT possess the moral courage or emotional strength to come alongside a wife who was being given catastrophic news that her husband was dead. *How in the heck would making a casserole or offering to clean her house make one iota of difference in a situation like that?* I was paralyzed with fear and worry.

These two days' worth of meetings and seminars were meant to help prepare those of us who were new to military life. The descriptions of acronyms and directions for navigating the "system" were meant to inform and assist. But I left the conference room both days with an ache in my heart, tears in my eyes, and a pain in the pit of my stomach.

My basic method of coping when I feel these conflicting emotions is to flee or escape. I made it back to Ryan's quarters that second day barely able to audibly articulate what I was feeling. It was time to cut bait with this Army commitment. It was time to tear up that contract, to say never mind. Couldn't we just say we'd had a change of heart? Surely there were others God could use or send. There was no way I was going to sacrifice my husband's life on the altar of national freedom. There was no way I could imagine that any sacrifices we could make as a family for America would ever be worth what our marriage would have to endure, what our kids would miss out on, and what we would deny ourselves in the comforts we loved and expected.

I was a bawling, crying mess. I just wanted to put the brakes on the move. Couldn't we simply get the moving truck to take our things back to our old parsonage? Surely it wasn't too late. I needed answers and for someone to help give our family an escape out of this madness. And the madness, well, it hadn't even truly begun.

I still remember asking Ryan why in the world we would give up so much for other people. I felt like Americans were generally so ungrateful and lacked understanding and like me, until two days before, had NO IDEA about the painful sacrifices military families made. How had I missed this information all of my life?

I asked Ryan how he felt at peace with laying down his life for his brother or for his country. In my emotionally disastrous meltdown I asked him how he could be willing to surrender his life for people he did not even know or people who may not even care or be aware of his sacrifice.

I realize my timing was terrible. To the average person, this new information would be the kind of counsel one would get *prior* to commissioning into active duty service, not the week before your first report date.

What He Needed:

I remember Ryan and I having several heated and tearful (again, me) discussions during this time. As many men are, Ryan is a fixer. He saw me upset and having a difficult time processing my emotions about it all and he wanted to offer a solution. I think he felt a certain sense of frustration with me early on about our decision and how distraught I was about everything we were giving up to fulfill God's calling. I was then and still am now, very selfish. I allow my flesh to often stand in the way of what I know the Lord has for me and where He longs to use me. You might even say I go kicking and screaming; well, kicking and crying is more like it.

Ryan's feelings of helplessness culminated that week of his graduation. As the primary provider for our family, I know he wanted to feel confident that we had made the right decision about our future. As the head of our household he wanted to take care of his family. He needed to know I felt proud of him and celebrated him during his graduation. I know it did much damage to Ryan to hear me losing it over making a casserole to take to a hypothetical new, young widow.

Ryan has known me long enough to know that I may have an affinity for blowing things way out of proportion but this time, he knew that I was seriously struggling. He knew that many of my concerns were valid.

He needed me to hold it together. He needed my support. He needed my encouragement and maybe even some excitement about our new adventure. And I, unfortunately, failed in every, single one of those areas.

I don't think it is healthy for us to fake it. We shouldn't have to sit on our ideas and feelings, but I do think I could have handled myself better during this time of transition. After all, timing is everything.

If I had it to do over again, I would try my best to convey my feelings to Ryan in a less emotional manner. I would try and talk through some of my thoughts on our transition a little bit here and a little bit there. I think there is wisdom in sharing what is on our hearts as it comes to us in small doses rather than having huge, *maybe-she-needs-a-straight-jacket-and-a-horse-tranquilizer* meltdowns.

During the CH-BOLC course, my contact with Ryan was limited, but if I had it to do over again, I think I would have tried sending him short email snippets with some of my concerns. I don't think they would have seemed so big and daunting to either of us, if they'd been spread out over the course of several weeks.

From My Blog: "Going Through the {e}Motions"

This has been a week full of charged emotions. From the excitement of our reunion, to the hustle and bustle of military balls, spouse seminars, and scheduled family activities, to the INFORMATION overload...I'm just about spent.

I don't want my blog to be a place where all I do is whine and fret, but it IS one place for me to let it all hang out and document our family story and journey.

We signed up for this I know. We agreed to this. We have made a commitment and there's no backing out. But I am nervous. Scared. Anxious. Happy. Excited. Sad. And mostly overwhelmed.

Ryan listened to me confess all of my worries for hours last night. It was a tearful night for me. The kind of crying where you are all stopped up. Can't breathe through your nose. Eyes red, huge, and puffy. You know, the ugly cry.

In my defense, I haven't had him to myself much this summer and I've been purposeful to avoid these type of meltdowns in front of others. But after all of the new information we were inundated with the past two days, my head has been full of thoughts and worries swimming around.

Number one. We are relocating in less than two weeks and we have nowhere to live. Every day I spend time looking on various websites and networks at possible housing options. We'll just have to wait and see when we get there. Post housing? What's available? Rentals? Not much to choose from that meets our criteria? Buy a house with record-low interest rates? Is this over-committing? Having a place to live and a physical address IS kind of a big deal, after all.

Number two. Spouse seminars. Ice breakers. Roles of a chaplain's spouse. Leadership and ministry opportunities. Military terms and acronyms. Introductions to customs and courtesies. Deployment. Reserve liaisons and unit mobilization. Staying connected during deployment. Family readiness. Religious pluralism. Tricare. Diversity in the military. Spouses' panel. Whew!

Seriously, I teared up at least twice yesterday during the spouses' seminar; thankfully, this is a supportive bunch. You hear suggestions on how to keep your family strong while Daddy is away for a year and see pictures and videos of soldiers hugging their kids they won't see for months on end. You hear things about how to minister to other wives who are 'keeping the home fires burning,' and how we as wives of chaplains have to support our husbands whose jobs require them to carry heavy emotional loads. They are fragile when they come home from a deployment or have to deliver news of the dead. You ask your husband why the dog tags he wears every day have one tag hanging lower than the other only to hear that the lower one is the 'toe tag,' used to identify a corpse. That's when you start really second guessing this whole, "Where You lead us Lord, we'll follow," idea that you gave yourselves to.

I literally said to Ryan the following last night: For six years our path led us toward serving in a church, a path upon which we originally thought we'd continue. Being a pastor (at least in our previous setting) meant that you were mostly around other Christians all of the time, and *even more so, like-minded Christians who believed the same things we do.*

Most of the sacrifices I thought I made then were sleeping in the floor at our annual youth retreat, Winterfest, or missing you for a week while you were in Honduras on a mission trip. And now we are going to be sacrificing months and even years of our time (and lives) AWAY from you; for me, my husband and the kids from their daddy?

But not just for the sake of the Gospel, but for Freedom...and for whom? Not our friends in our old church or maybe a new convert that may pass through our church doors once or twice a year, but for WHOM? Strangers. Why on Earth would we actually WANT to do this? Why would we sacrifice all of these things for people we don't even know?

And you want to know what Ryan said? He played the Jesus card. He said, "Isn't that what Jesus did?" Aren't we supposed to follow the Great Commission to go and make disciples of all men (and women)? Not just the ones like us or geographically near to us, but all nations (Matthew 28:19).

Yes, Ryan. You are right. We are. But this is the part where I shamefully admitted my own selfishness. And it's a big, huge, all-about-me-and-mine selfishness. Maybe in my own strength I am not cut out for this life of sacrifice after all.

God, I need You to help make me able. God, I'm counting on You to never leave me or forsake me. Equip me to do this job.

God's Use for the Trial:

After nearly a full year of going through the commissioning process and Ryan's initial training, the Lord finally, graciously gave me the reminder I needed. It culminated that night at the Fort Jackson Inn in Ryan's suite. Basically it came down to a personal reflection and crisis of my own faith. If this command is good enough for Jesus, shouldn't it be good enough for me?

We didn't exactly *choose* this journey. We allowed ourselves to be open to the Lord's leading for our lives and for our family. And He alone ordained the steps to get us here. He opened doors and made the way possible. And there is no denying His handprints all over the process it took for Ryan to get picked up as an active duty chaplain.

In my angst over the lack of appreciation that others show toward the sacrifices of military families, it came to me, that when we choose to lay down our lives for our families and when our husbands choose to take an oath to defend and honor our country and its freedoms, we are taking an active step toward living out the commands and the mission of Jesus Christ.

As Believers we seek to model the ways of Christ in our own lives. As military folks, we get to put this principle into practice with our livelihoods. God reminds us that through our military service we are living according to His purposes.

"Greater love have no man than this, that someone lay down his life for his friends." {John 15:13}

A mission
ready marriage
says, "Here I
am Lord, send
me . . ."

Questions for Reflection:

1. Describe your own personal experience of getting involved in military life. Any prior associations before you were married?

2. Did you ever have any initial "kicking and screaming" (or crying) moments at the outset? If so, please explain.

3. Looking back, can you see that God had a purpose for calling you to military life? Are there any "handprints" you find when you relate to your own story?

4. Did anything in your early military involvement put a wedge in your marriage? Was there any tension between you and your spouse regarding his service or commitment to duty? How did you overcome this?

5. What are your thoughts on the correlation between God's calling to each of us to show "greater love..." by laying down our lives (our plans and our wishes for what WE want in life) for the greater good of our "friends," (strangers, fellow Americans, freedom for all)?

Chapter 2

Homesickness and Longing for What Once Was

People find their way into military life for a vast array of reasons. Some enlist right out of high school. For some it is a natural progression from an ROTC program or the family tradition. Many use the military as a means for paying for college and for some, it is literally a last resort and a place to run to for those with no plan or prospects for their futures.

As spouses, some arrive to the military already married; others marry into this organization. And yet, still some have an entirely different life or set of circumstances prior to their association with the armed forces. However one arrives at this destination through marriage, we all have something or someone we leave behind to pursue this wandering, nomadic life. We all have a home of origin somewhere that existed long before we said "I Do" to Uncle Sam.

I grew up and lived my first three decades of life in a medium size, metropolitan city in southeast Tennessee. Chattanooga is the perfect city. Geographically there are mountains and the beautiful Tennessee River runs right through the landscape. There are hills and valleys, multiple bodies of water, and plenty of places to enjoy the outdoors. In Chattanooga, you get all four seasons of the year; a fact I took for granted until we moved away.

There is plenty of night life and culture; there is a rich history predating the American Civil War and a tapestry of urbanization that has always dominated Chattanooga. It really is an awesome place to call home.

The fact that my entire extended family is in the surrounding area and suburbs of Chattanooga makes a physical place even more special to me. Nearly every memory of my life was made in Chattanooga, save for a few vacations every year when we would travel out of state to go to the beach or to the mountains.

I have always held a deep sense of longing for place, for home. Chattanooga embodies nearly every aspect of that idea for me. My family is there. My memories are there. My roots are there. A piece of my heart will always be there. It will come as no surprise that leaving this fair city was somewhat traumatic for me. I began to long for it even before we left.

In January of 2011, just before we packed up and moved out of our parsonage and a few months before Ryan began CH-BOLC, we received paper orders in the mail from Fort Knox. We were so incredibly naive we believed that opening that envelope would reveal to us one of the three choices we had listed on our proverbial dream sheet.

Being so attached to Chattanooga and our families, Ryan and I prayerfully listed Fort Benning, (Columbus, Georgia), Fort Campbell (Clarksville, Tennessee), and Fort Bragg (Fayetteville, North Carolina). We eagerly ripped open the envelope to see which of those three places the Army picked for us. Hilarious, right?

We were such dummies! We had no clue that the "needs of the Army" trumped any suggestions or requests we might catalog on a preference list or dream sheet. You can imagine our surprise to find orders for Ryan to be assigned as a battalion/squadron chaplain for the First Armored Division at Fort Bliss (El Paso, TX). I actually had to Google Fort Bliss because I had never even heard of it, much less ever considered it as the place the Army would send us on our first assignment.

After Googling the location of Fort Bliss, my next step was to open up Google Maps and calculate the driving distance between Chattanooga, Tennessee and El Paso, Texas. I will not repeat here the words that I whispered when I realized that we would be moving *ONE THOUSAND, FOUR HUNDRED, TWENTY-ONE* miles from the only home we had ever known.

I knew the move to Texas was inevitable. I mistakenly believed that the Lord would see fit to keep us as close to home as possible. I figured God knew my need to ease gently into military life by remaining near our home of origin. Surely He understood it would make this a less painful assimilation by allowing us to be near our families.

Ryan, the kids, and I went out to our favorite Mexican restaurant that night to celebrate our news and "celebrate" the new culture we would be a part of in El Paso. In case you didn't know this, as I didn't at the time, El Paso, Texas is located on the United States/Mexico border at Ciudad Juarez.

It took me two full days of letting the news sink in before I had the courage to call my parents to tell them where we were moving. The memory of calling my folks with the news is still vivid to me. I had to screw my courage to the sticking place and strengthen my resolve. It would be the first of many times to come for putting on my Big Girl Panties (BGP). It was time to let my mom and dad in on the location of our assignment. My dad answered the phone but I had him get my mom on the other line in another room in their house so I could tell them both at once. I was justifiably afraid I would lose my nerve if I had to say "*El Paso*" and "*1,400 miles*" a second time. No sooner than I got those words out of my mouth, my poor dad asked, "*Well, who do we need to call to get that changed?*"

You see, my dad, a civilian, with absolutely no military experience was not wise to the operations of the Army. We laugh about it now, but there never was nor will there ever be a phone call to be made to get your duty assignment switched. It may be the way the real world works when you are connected and know people. It is definitely not the way the military works. Sweet Dad.

Almost immediately, I began my research on El Paso. I began using the Internet as a way to find Texas equivalents to our Chattanooga life. Instantly I was perusing zip codes and school ratings, extra-curricular activities via church websites, Chamber of Commerce suggestions of things to do, as well as cultural offerings like museums and theaters. From my preliminary Internet research, my heart was already breaking. It turns out El Paso is nothing like Chattanooga. It didn't take much searching online to realize that!

Ryan had driven out immediately following his CH-BOLC graduation with my father-in-law who graciously drove my loaded down vehicle. Ryan was ahead of us by about a week. The kids and I arrived in El Paso on August 30, 2011, our youngest daughter, Kate's, fourth birthday. We flew to El Paso and arrived just in time for dinner. I still remember walking out of the airport and being in awe of the high desert sky. It dawned on me that we were two time zones west of where we had left that morning. In reality, we were a world away. Ryan did his best to turn a long day of flights and airports into a cozy, festive welcome to our new city.

We had dinner at Julio's Cafe and Corona and tasted the first of many authentic Mexican dishes. The next month was spent in very close quarters at the Army Hotel on main post. Our options for post housing were few and after realizing there would be an 18 month wait time, we immediately found a realtor and decided to purchase a home. It took several weeks for the inspections, closing and paperwork to get handled but by the end of September, we had settled into our new space at Redstone Pass Court.

For the previous six years we had lived in a fifty year old church parsonage with chocolate brown appliances. It looked like a kitchen that Betty Draper would have used; straight out of Mad Men. I was so thrilled to have our own home again, a place that was truly ours. Ryan was with us again, the kids and I were out of the extra bedrooms at my parents' house and we were finally free after a 36 night stay in a standard hotel room with five people.

As we were getting our household goods delivered and put away, the reality of our situation was truly sinking in. We were in a new house, in a new town...literally a thousand miles from nowhere. The adjustment period was intense.

I had begun homeschooling the kids only weeks before our move. Ryan spent his days at his new job teeming with new colleagues and I was home alone in a new town getting my bearings in my brand new role as mother/teacher/military spouse. I still remember getting out and going for a drive in those early weeks. I was honked at not once but twice and shown that I was "number one," with the middle finger. I broke down in tears.

Having traveled the same roads, highways, and routes for my entire life, it was extremely daunting to not know where I was going on any given day. I didn't know where to go eat, where the best grocery stores were, where to get our hair cut, our teeth cleaned, which pharmacy was best, or where to find friends for me or our three children.

We were making phone calls back home almost every day and it took all I had not to cry on the phone with my parents, in-laws, and close friends. I knew there would be an adjustment period. I just didn't know how long it might take.

Prior to leaving Chattanooga, I was so well-connected and plugged in. I played in a Bunco group with girls from my old elementary school. I had a book club full of my teaching buddies from my first job right out of college. I had mom friends in multiple circles; those from pre-school, those from my son's elementary school, those from our church and another church in town where I attended Moms of Pre-Schoolers (MOPS). The same girl had cut my hair for almost a decade, my dentist was the only one I had ever known, I had a library card to the library of my childhood, and I could navigate my way around my stomping grounds with my eyes closed.

Being new in town, I had none of that. In fact, other than my immediate family and this new house, I felt like I had said goodbye to EVERYTHING and presently had NOTHING! The only thing I had an abundance of, was tears. And I cried and cried and cried. I cried in the shower, in the car, in bed with my back to Ryan. I sat in my closet and cried. I walked the sidewalks of my new neighborhood and cried. I called my sister and cried. I cried to one of only a handful of new friends I met, another chaplain's wife from the South, Kelly. She knew how hard is was to be this far away from home and she met me with such grace and kindness.

I felt an immense and intense pressure to make it and survive. I did not want to admit defeat so soon, but I continued to doubt if I was going to be okay in El Paso. I tried to hold it together as much as possible in front of the kids, but there were times when I cried in front of them too.

What I Needed:

During those first months, I needed to feel validated. I needed someone to say, *"Claire, you are right, it is hard. This thing you are doing is not for the faint of heart. This crazy, cross-country move, this uprooting and replanting is difficult."* I needed to be able to let those tears fall. I know that they were precious to God. Looking back I know they were tears of surrender.

I also needed to feel a sense of belonging in my new city and surroundings. What it took me a while to realize was that what I had in Chattanooga by way of family and a life, had literally taken a lifetime to build. The investments I had made in people and places were not able to be recreated in an instant. I knew deep down that it would be a process and that it would take time to feel settled and to feel a sense of community and belonging. In hindsight, I should have allowed myself that grace. I should have given myself the green light to grieve a little and then begin laying a foundation for friendships and connections. Instead, I excessively wallowed in self-pity.

Some of what helped was finding a few places to plug in for myself and for our three children. I began going to every spouses' coffee and event I was invited to. If someone showed me any kindness, I really took notice, tried to be a friend, and made myself available for new friendships and relationships. I attended an on-post women's Bible study, Protestant Women of the Chapel (PWOC), we found a family friendly chapel service, and I registered the kids for a homeschool co-op as well as a homeschool golf class every Tuesday after lunch.

These new people I was meeting weren't replacements for my mom or sister or girlfriends I had known half of my life. However, I needed contact with face to face friends. I needed to begin making inroads with other ladies who were walking this military journey. I needed heart connections and I needed to be sure there were like-minded people around us to walk through the challenges and joys of life in El Paso.

As someone who is notoriously impatient, I did not want to wait for those pieces to all fall into place. I wanted to transfer my lifetime of feeling connected, known, and relationally secure to a new city with the snap of my finger. The Lord would soon teach me patience and total reliance upon Him.

What He Needed:

During this time, Ryan had a big learning curve with his assimilation into military life in general, chaplaincy, and life in a cavalry squadron that was already in the midst of pre-deployment training. He needed more of my support than I think I was honestly able to give to him.

He needed to be able to come home from work and simply be. He needed our home to be a peaceful place of rest and relaxation. He also needed to be able to sleep at bedtime. On more occasions than I care to admit, I would sulk and pout throughout the late afternoon and evening when Ryan would return from a long day at work. He would ask if I was okay, or "*What's wrong?*" And I would expect him to have supernatural mind-reading powers. Saying you are fine when you really aren't is unfair to you and your spouse. That omission of truth can ruin many an evening at home.

Frequently I would wait until Ryan was just about ready to turn off his bedside lamp and doze off, to hit him with an outburst of tears, emotions, and *all of my feelings*! I would lament our old life. I would cry, sniffle, and espouse my dissatisfaction with this new city and this new place. I would bare my heartbreak over what I was missing, what the kids were missing, and how I just could not seem to feel plugged in no matter how hard I tried. I missed our old friends and our families. Even our old dilapidated parsonage was holding some appeal in my memory and in my heart. I missed my old job as a part-time college English instructor, our pediatrician, and my kids' teachers. I longed for the familiar.

I would keep Ryan up all hours of the night until I had worked myself into what he affectionately calls "*a tizzy*." I would finally get my sinuses so stopped up from crying that I would begin to hyperventilate a little and then I would crash from the sheer exhaustion of carrying around all of these burdensome emotions.

Ryan needed me to just breathe and give it time. He needed me to take a step back and take a glance at the blessings surrounding us. He needed me to hunt the good stuff.

If I had it to do over, I would simmer way down. I would chill out and realize Rome wasn't built in day and neither would a life in Texas. I would be rational and remember that constructing a new life in a new place would not be an overnight event. It would take time and I would need to be patient with the process.

In our past life, the comforts I had grown to love were the product of three decades worth of living. How foolish of me to expect instantaneous assimilation into El Paso life and Army life too!

From My Blog: "We're Not in Kansas Anymore"

Or alternately titled, "I'm So Homesick," or "I've Cried at Some Point Every Day During the Past Four Days," or "Pity Party Alert," or "You Try Living In a Hotel for 25 Days and See How Your Emotions Are Holding Out." You can take your pick on one of these titles because any or all of them would suffice.

I'm not in a depression or anything other than what I believe to be the normal stages of this kind of grief. The excitement and novelty of living in a new place has certainly worn off. Everything here is different. Everything. Army life is different. Living away from my family and Ryan's is different. Churches and chapel services are different. The people are different. The geography is different. The culture is different. Being a new homeschooler is even different.

I know that different can be good, but so far, different is just different. And awkward. And lonely. I am really trusting that the Lord is going to come through BIG TIME and SOON! I know He'll prove Himself faithful just as He has always done. In weeks and months ahead I'll look back and read this and think, "How silly," or "Remember when we just got here and how things were?"

I cried Sunday after chapel service. I cried at lunch at Cracker Barrel sitting outside in the rockers listening to country music songs. It made me think of my Tennessee roots. I think it was the Moon-Pies on the shelves and seeing the "Manufactured in Chattanooga," that did me in.

47

I cried in bed that night while the rest of my family was sleeping. I cried Monday when I saw a matchy-matchy mother/daughter duo. I KNOW these people are homeschoolers. They were leaving the library when we were getting there. Pretty soon, Mae, Kate and I will be growing out our hair, wearing long French-braids and I'll be sewing us matching outfits. Is this what we're becoming? I cried Monday night at dinner. We were at eating at Chili's and the kids pointed out the Molten Chocolate Cake. It made me think of my parents. My dad always ordered one for the kids when we'd eat out together. I cried yesterday driving around. Lost.

And then again when someone laid on his horn at me for pulling out in front of his car. We spent most of the day out running errands and staying busy. I try not to let the kids see me crying like a little baby. It's mostly just tears rolling down my face anyway, not an all-out boo-hoo-hoo.

I am such a creature of habit and the familiar and we have none of that right now. No habits. No familiar. I just miss my family. Ryan's family. All of my friends. The kids' friends. Our sports. Our schools. Northgate Mall, the library, the post office, the 153 Target, Publix, and Hixson Pike. I miss good praise and worship music in a church setting, mountains, trees, our house, our belongings and our Chattanooga life. There. I said it. Moving on.

The Lord continues to show me more of Himself daily. His strength is perfect. His grace is sufficient. His mercies are new every morning.

God's Use for the Trial:

I truly believe that God uses every situation He allows in our lives for His glory and His good. While I know that He placed me into my family of origin, in my home town for a distinct purpose, He also took me away from that for a specific reason and He did that for my growth.

The blessing of family and the familiar is a wonderful thing. But I had begun to make a god out of my comfort. I had begun to see living near my family in the world's best city as a means of control and as an idol that was crowding my heart. I erroneously believed that my need for my siblings, parents, and extended family nearby was greater than my need to be in the will of God.

I wrongly believed that in areas where my marriage was weak, the voids I felt there could be filled with all the friendships, activities, and connections of living in Chattanooga. For the first time in our then, almost ten year marriage, I had to finally stand on my own two feet. Ryan and I both had to cut the proverbial (umbilical) cord. I had come to a very real and tangible place in my life where I had to put my money where my mouth was, or put feet to my faith, so to speak.

I said I was a Christ-follower. I said I wanted to be in God's good, perfect, and pleasing will, but did I mean it? Was I willing to take up His cross at *all* costs?

Until this point in my life, I had easily passed all the trials and tests of my faith. Sure I had questioned, doubted, and wondered where God was during difficult times. But our move to El Paso put me in a geographical place where my faith was in sink or swim mode. I had to decide in both my head and heart if what I said I believed about following Jesus was true for me. Was I willing to follow Him only when it was safe, comfortable, and convenient or was I willing to follow Him even to the ends of the Earth (or in our case, the ends and borderlands of the United States)?

Would I be willing to forego my plans and wishes for a specific place to live at the cost of taking up His cross and giving our lives to His service and in service to our country?

I can say in all honesty, this was not a clear cut answer for me. I knew it needed to be, but the peace in this decision or the answer to these questions wasn't so immediate. It took me months of pouring out my heart to the Lord and months of processing and articulating this faith passage to close friends and mentors to really feel clear about it in my heart.

I knew God had called us to this work and therefore, I knew He ordained our footsteps and guided us straight to Fort Bliss in El Paso, Texas. I believe we are all afflicted with a sense of homesickness. Maybe it is for family or a particular city, but deep, deep down in the recesses of our souls, it is a homesickness for eternity and for peaceful rest in the Father's will. God reminds us that no duty assignment or earthly city is the home of our hearts.

"But our citizenship is in heaven, and from it we await a Savior, the Lord Jesus Christ, who will transform our lowly body to be like His glorious body, by the power that enables Him even to subject all things to Himself." {*Philippians 3:20-21*}

A mission ready marriage realizes that this world is not our home.

Questions for Reflection:

1. Where was your first duty assignment and what were your initial reactions about the location? Did you mourn leaving your hometown behind or were you ready to flee from there and start over?

2. Was this assignment on your "dream sheet?" Why or why not? What have been your experiences with "dream assignments" or locations?

3. Did any of your reactions to settling in at the new assignment put any tensions on your marriage? If so, how?

4. What memory stands out the most to you as a faith-building trial in your new town? Did you feel lost? Or lacking in a particular area? How did you see or feel God provide? How long did that process take?

5. Looking back, explain some of the specific ways God ministered to you during this time. How did you get through it? What advice would you give someone new coming into that particular location?

Chapter 3

Leaving and Cleaving

I grew up in a very loving, functional family. I am the oldest of three children. I have a brother three years younger than me and a sister six years younger. My parents were high school sweethearts and have been married for over forty years. They remained in the town where they grew up (Chattanooga), and never lived more than 10 or 15 miles from either set of my grandparents.

One of my grandfathers pastored the same church for over 17 years, the other spent more than two decades working in the same nylon and textiles plant. Longevity runs in my family.

My dad has worked his entire professional career for the same bank. Although the ownership has changed a handful of times, my dad has remained a faithful employee and hard worker. He has continued to stay relevant and needed in an ever changing industry. He will be retiring soon and none of us know what he is going to do with himself when he doesn't have to wear a starched button-down shirt and tie, suit, and wingtip shoes every day.

My mom has worked as an orthodontic assistant since before I was born. In her forty plus year tenure, she has worked for exactly three orthodontists. She has been with her most recent boss, for over twenty-five years. My mom has remained a faithful and hard-working employee; she even put braces on all three of her kids! My first paid job was working for the dentist who practiced right next door to the office where my mom worked. The summer after my tenth grade school year, my mom and I rode to and from work together.

My siblings and I had a very steady and blessed childhood. We were raised in church; the same one my dad grew up in as a pastor's son. All three of us had the same teachers and graduated from the same high school. My dad still has all of our letterman jackets, pom-poms, yearbooks, academic and sports highlight reels preserved at their house. Our high school years were some of my dad's favorite times.

We shopped at the same Gap at Northgate Mall for our back to school clothes every year, ate after church lunches at the same Piccadilly Cafeteria, and got our groceries from the same Red Food Store (BiLo) every week.

At different intervals over the years I have asked my parents if they ever considered moving away from Chattanooga. Really, they never seriously considered it. To them, Chattanooga is home. Their parents and extended families are there, their steady jobs are there, their whole life is there. Why would they ever leave?

When Ryan and I started dating, we were both out of college. I had begun my teaching career in Cleveland, TN (less than half an hour north of Chattanooga). This is the same town where Ryan had gone to Lee University and lived back at home with his parents. He had pursued a bachelor's degree in biology. A very wonderful, but useless major for finding employment. When we met, Ryan was running the pro-shop at a golf course where he had worked since he was in high school. As our relationship evolved, he got back in school and began to pursue graduate studies to gain a teaching certificate. We had plans for a future together and he knew he needed a legitimate career path in mind if my parents were going to consider Ryan's interest in me seriously.

We dated during my first year of teaching. Ryan patiently sat with me for hours on school bleachers as I sponsored the varsity cheerleading squad. By my second year teaching, we were engaged. I had started graduate school and Ryan had finished his Master's degree securing his own teaching and coaching job at the rival school across town.

Once we were married, it seemed that we would stay in Cleveland as we both had good jobs and Ryan's dad (a general contractor) had begun construction on a beautiful, custom home for us only a few miles up the road from Ryan's family homestead.

Our plans for this home, our marriage, and future together looked very predictable. In our hearts, as far as we could see or imagine, we just knew we would both put in 30 year teaching careers at our respective schools and bring home all of our future babies to this house. We planned to raise them there. We would firmly establish ourselves and put down family roots of our own. We wanted longevity to run in our family too.

Over the course of the next several years, Ryan and I did have some transitions, however. After our first child, Thomas, was born, I left my full-time teaching job for good. I began adjunct teaching at my alma-mater, (University of Tennessee at Chattanooga) and my mom and grandmother helped care for Thomas the few mornings each week I had classes. Ryan left his teaching and coaching job after about four years. He enrolled in a Master of Divinity program and we moved back to Chattanooga to work full-time as the youth pastors of my childhood church where my parents attended.

At the time, we assumed that since teaching careers were off the table, God had placed on our hearts to serve in full-time, pastoral ministry. All of the right doors opened and we spent the next six years mostly happy to be right where we were. We brought our second child, Mae, home and less than two years after that, our family was complete with the birth of our third child, Kate.

Life was good. Our family was complete. We had both sets of doting grandparents nearby to help with occasional babysitting. They attended our kids' pre-school performances and little league sports. Our lives were firmly entrenched in theirs and theirs in ours.

You can imagine their surprise when the Lord moved in our hearts in 2010 and placed in us a burden to minister to the military. As Believers, all of our parents were fully supportive of our mission; but selfishly they hated to see us uproot ourselves from the familiar.

It was these deep and tangled roots that made it especially difficult for Ryan and me to move away too. Ultimately we knew our calling to the U.S. Army was a calling only the Lord could have put in our hearts and we ultimately chose to walk in obedience to Him.

As typical first-born children, Ryan and I are both pleasers. Even as grown adults, we value our parents' blessing and approval of our life and choices. We still seek their wisdom and advice when we face major decisions. As wonderful role models, followers of Jesus, and sacrificial parents all four, they have earned that respect.

When our journey into the Army and away from Chattanooga got real, Ryan and I were left staring at each other wondering what we were supposed to do now? For the first time in our entire lives we were really, finally, and wholly on our own. We didn't have our parents nearby to influence us, instruct us or even occasionally guilt us into doing things.

As strange as it sounds, we, at the ripe ages of 34, had finally gained true independence from our parents. It was thrilling, sobering, and confounding all at the same time. Having *so much* connection with our folks, we often allowed them to call the shots on certain aspects of our lives. They graciously and generously planned and treated us to family vacations. They even blessed us financially on a few occasions during our leanest seminary years. At the heart of it, their motives were always to bless us and show us love and support.

Once our boots hit the ground in El Paso, we felt like we had finally grown up in an instant. I realize for most people, this rite of passage comes when a person goes away to college or gets married and moves away. For Ryan and me, this moment came nearly ten years into our marriage.

What I Needed:

During those first several months of our relocation, it felt new to me to rely on Ryan so much as the leader of our home. Even amidst my own emotional struggles to find my footing in Army life, homeschooling life, and El Paso life I *was* standing on my own two feet. Despite this new found independence, I was feeling very lonely and I needed Ryan's reassurance.

Thankfully Ryan is a very realistic, levelheaded, and positive person. He reminded me at every turn that it was the Lord who had called us and it would be the Lord that sustained us.

I still remember only a few months in that I had gotten very concerned about when we might be able to afford or take the time off to travel back to Tennessee. I knew from the outset of our move, that air travel for five was costly. The kids and I had recently flown out to El Paso in late August. The price those four expensive tickets was still fresh in my mind and in our checkbook.

Air travel alone with a (then) four, five and seven year old was also daunting. I reasoned that I couldn't handle a twenty-three hour car ride with the kids by myself. Ryan had acquired very little time off and was unsure about how much leave he would have built up during that first holiday season.

In my typical, hopeless, the-glass-is-half-empty, Debby Downer mindset, I just assumed that once we moved to Texas, we would almost NEVER, EVER, EVER get to see our families again. It felt permanent. It felt like when we told them all goodbye, we were going to never be part of their lives again. Ryan reminded me that there would be opportunities to eventually travel back to Tennessee.

Only fifteen weeks after we had arrived in El Paso, Ryan bought plane tickets for the kids and me to fly home in time to celebrate my extended family's annual weekend at a chalet in the Great Smoky Mountains. Ryan made the trip by car a week later when his unit had block leave. We spent two whole weeks with our families and drove back to El Paso together at the end of December.

Ryan knew I needed to see not just our families. He knew I needed to see the possibility and the reality that despite complicated, costly, and long travel we *would* travel back. We *could* travel back. We would stay connected. Family is forever, even if it takes a few days to get home.

What He Needed:

Ryan needed to let me let *him* lead. He needed me to stop trying to micro-manage our lives, our calendars, and all of the major and minute details of everything. He also needed me to trust him.

I think for so long, I had misguided trust in my parents and in-laws. It was not necessarily a conscious intention, but for the first ten years of our marriage, I was looking for the approval and direction of our family to ultimately come from the generations before us to tell us what to do. In a way, it was a lack of trust and full confidence in Ryan's role as head of our household.

Because he is typically so laid back and easy-going, I think we had both inadvertently allowed other substantial influences to dominate our marriage. It was time to let Ryan steer our ship. He had been well prepared. He had been raised in a loving home with wonderful parents and Christian role models all around.

Ryan has always treated me with love and respect. He has always cherished me and put my needs and often my wants above his own. It was time for me to realize that and see that he and I were not at odds. No, not at all. We were on the same team. We had the same dreams, hopes, and a cohesive vision of our ministry calling.

He needed me to realize that he wanted the best for me, our children, our ministry, and our future. I think I knew that truth deep down somewhere, but I had kept a wall up. I had allowed a false sense of security in our parents, (even as adults, and even as well-meaning as they all were) to become what counted the most.

Husbands want to feel honored and cherished. When we look to other influences, even good ones, as substitutes for their leadership, it can lead us down a negative path. Ryan doesn't demand that I lean on him. His love toward me makes me want to rely on his wisdom, initiative, and good judgment.

It was time to cast my vote of confidence in my husband. We are partners and a team unit. There is no one on this Earth that I would rather move all over the country with. I have a great husband. And I am glad to be on his team as we navigate Army life and ministry together.

From My Blog: "What I Love About Ryan"

It goes without saying that Ryan is my heart, my love, my partner, my other (better) half. The longer we are married the more we realize that standing at the altar taking our vows, we didn't really, truly know one another. Yes, we dated over a year and had an eight month engagement, but in many ways we have grown up with each other throughout our marriage. Through both the highs and lows, the joys and trials we have had one another to lean on. I know that is how God intended for it to be.

When it comes to temperament and personality, I am definitely more of the open-book, sanguine of the two. Ryan is a classic introvert, a man of few words, someone who needs time to think over things and hold them inside. He is rational, level-headed, determined, laid-back...basically all of the things I am not.

Ryan will probably cringe when he reads all of these platitudes and compliments about himself. Why? Well, because that's just Ryan. He doesn't like the spotlight or attention or glory. His humility and selflessness are hallmarks of his personality and I think that's why he is thriving so well in a job that is marked by service to others, to God, and to country.

Over the course of our marriage I have learned that Ryan can do anything. I grew up with a wonderful dad who despite his lack of technical, handy-man skills had the discretionary income to just pay for what was needed for repairs, for installations, and every manner of car and home maintenance. I love my Dad and just about everyone who knows him knows the running joke about his "toolbox." We also knew as kids if a toy needed assembly or if something was broken, Mom was our first line of defense. She'd at least had the wherewithal to keep assembly directions and make an attempt. My mom is definitely the Bob Vila of that duo.

Back to Ryan. When we married, I never knew of anyone to change his own oil in a vehicle? I never knew (seriously) of seeing someone pull out the television to maneuver wires and hookups and get different components working. I certainly never saw anyone build something with his bare hands. Ryan is nothing if not industrious. He has not only changed oil in our vehicles, he has put on brakes, repaired window motors, and I think he could probably rotate our tires if he had the equipment.

He has helped roof a house (one of our former church parsonages), he's built things on mission trips, he's handled plumbing issues, he's even dabbled in woodworking. He made his own desk and podium when he taught school. He even crafted miniature wooden bunk beds for Mae and Kate's American Girl dolls. Ryan has repaired boat motors, sodded our yard, killed and grown his own food. He has single-handedly taught himself how to play the guitar and banjo.

I know this is starting to sound ridiculous, but before we had smart phones with GPS and Google, he has navigated his way all over the country with nary a map. I think he can tell time by looking at the sun. So basically I married MacGyver. And if Ryan doesn't instinctively know something, he will teach himself how to do it. He will study a *problem and devise a solution. (See above with that whole patient, level-headed, determined thing...) Add to that list, Ryan is great golfer, handsome, well read...and well, I think we're talking about a true Renaissance man. When I reflect on it, about the only things he can't do well are ride roller blades gracefully or cut a rug out on the dance floor.*

Most recently when Ryan mentioned that he wanted to make a lift/contraption/pulley (I forget the real name of it) to be able to remove the hard top from his Jeep and store it in our garage, I didn't even bat an eye. Of course he wanted to. If I've learned anything in these years of marriage, it's that Ryan has got skills. Give him a tape measure and a drill and sit back and prepare to be amazed.

He spent hours researching the methods and materials and in true Ryan style, he sketched out a little blueprint and made his rounds to Lowe's and Harbor Freight. I came out to the garage to see the progress and I literally watched Ryan finger a rope for about three minutes to figure out what type of knot he needed to use. I could see his mind just working away to get this right.

He measured twice, cut once and in about two work sessions and $75 later, his masterpiece was complete. He can back into the garage and use the winch to lift and store the hard top. I think that this kind of industry and ingenuity is a lost art. Few men are teaching their sons how to be self-sufficient and fixers. I'm thankful that Ryan comes from a long line of men who know how to find solutions to problems. Ryan, I love you and I have been too often guilty of not acknowledging or appreciating the gift-of-you that's right in front of me.

God's Use for the Trial:

Not everyone has the same family background that Ryan and I have. I fully realize the blessing of having supportive parents who are still married and living their lives following after Jesus, is unlikely the norm. My background sounds idyllic or too good to be true. After all, often times people grow up in homes and family situations that they are ready to flee from as soon as they can get out of the house.

There is dysfunction, turmoil, abuse and the very last thing a person wants to do is stay connected to his/her family of origin. However, growing up in the stability and steadfastness that we did, Ryan and I are unusually close to ours. We still joke at the fact that when Ryan asked my parents for my hand in marriage, my dad gave his (and my mom's) blessing but offered Ryan that if I ever became too much for him to handle (my dad had a lifetime of experience with my crying, emotions, and sensitivity), that he was free to bring me back home. My dad told Ryan I would always have a place with him and my mom.

It took the Army sending Ryan and me halfway across the country *away* from our parents through a physical and geographical separation to cut the ties. Without the comforts of our families and close friends, we were left alone to embark on our new adventure together with our own children. There had not necessarily been a failure to launch prior to our first Army assignment. We just hadn't known any other way.

The Lord graciously used this time for us to literally reset our marriage. We began with new expectations of one another. We relied on the wisdom and perspectives of the other's strengths. We were really, finally following the Biblical mandate of becoming "*one flesh.*"

This was the way God intended marriage to function all along. In His Providence, He gave Ryan and me the push we needed to realize once and for all, that God alone ordained our relationship and partnership. Christ was our leader and in whom we placed our trust to follow Him wherever He may lead us. As long as we are together in spirit, I knew we would be together (and okay) during times we were physically apart. This revelation came all too soon. Almost immediately upon our arrival to Fort Bliss, Ryan's unit began training up for a swiftly approaching deployment to Operation Enduring Freedom (OEF) in Afghanistan. I am grateful for the time we had to re-establish our foundation and priorities as a couple and family before an event of such magnitude affected us.

From the beginning, God's plan and purpose was for a man and woman to be joined together in unity and begin their lives and covenant relationship afresh and anew. We are to leave behind the ties of our parents and separate from them. We are to cleave to one another as husband and wife.

"Therefore a man shall leave his father and his mother and hold fast to his wife, and they shall become one flesh." {*Genesis 2:24*}

A mission ready marriage knows when it is time to leave and cleave.

Questions for Reflection:

1. Briefly describe your family of origin. What kind of home did you grow up in? What about your husband? Was his upbringing similar to your own or vastly different? Has this ever caused disagreements or opposing points of view on major issues? If yes, please explain.

2. When did you *really* leave home for the first time? Is there anything in particular about your family that made it especially difficult OR easy to leave them?

3. Does your husband have any special qualities or unique characteristics that make it notably easy or difficult to allow him to lead your home? Please elaborate.

4. What are your thoughts on the idea of "leaving and cleaving?" How has life in the military forced you to "cleave" to your spouse and rely on him more? Can you cite a specific instance when this was particularly true?

5. If your marriage still is not on sure footing, what are some practical and realistic steps you could take to help establish a tighter bond or stronger ties with your spouse?

Chapter 4
Home is Where the Army Sends Us: Broken Furniture and Mending Dreams

The nicest house Ryan and I have ever lived in was actually our very first house. With all of his connections in the construction industry, many of Ryan's dad's colleagues donated their time and materials to help build Ryan and me our dream home. We had over 2,200 finished square feet plus another 1,200 unfinished square feet of basement. There were three garage bays, an enormous wrap around front porch, tons of beautiful finishes and moldings, as well as plantation wooden blinds on our windows. This home at Anderson Cabin Road was really a labor of love from Ryan's parents. We hated to sell what we assumed would be our forever home after living there only a few short years.

From there Ryan and I lived in our parsonage, the oldest of all of the houses we have lived in. Our church's campus had relocated to what had previously been a 30 acre family farm. The church facility was built on a prime portion the land and there were three existing brick ranch-style homes that had survived since the 1960s.

In their prime these homes were very nice and furnished with top of the line fixtures. There were lavish mirrored doors, brown Kitchen Aid appliances, a big brick fireplace, a spacious patio, all wood window frames and the piece de' resistance was the (no longer operational) sound system that was wired through every room in the house. We had three full bathrooms and three large bedrooms.

All of the bedrooms were on one end of the house and we enjoyed having separate living areas with both a formal living/dining room and den. This house was full of windows and wonderful light. Out our back door was a large, open field. Every Easter our church held a community egg hunt there. But for the other 364 days each year, we pretended that was our very own back yard. Our kids played for hours in that space with their baseball bats and gloves, electric Jeep, and soccer ball.

Every year we planted a garden in that back yard and fed countless birds with our bird feeders. We enjoyed more than one big snow where lots of friends and family came over and we all took turns pulling each other in make-shift sleds anchored to four-wheelers. As Southerners, we often prefer wild thrills over safety.

We lived where we worked and on many days, that was annoying. It seemed we were always unlocking the church for someone who needed the fellowship hall or had forgotten something. But far outweighing the hassles, we welcomed so many people into our home during those six years. This house was a huge blessing to us while we resided there.

We held student gatherings and progressive dinners, hosted baby showers, Thanksgivings, birthday parties, game nights, couples' fellowships, Bunco, book club, and breakfast with Santa.

I still remember one unseasonably cold Easter where the temperatures were below freezing. I invited all of the young moms and their nearly frost-bitten kids into our house in lieu of catching hypothermia at the egg hunt. To this day, I consider my retired next door neighbor Lou, (who also lived on the church grounds) one of my dearest friends. We would share leftovers and often spend many afternoons chatting together.

That house taught us a most valuable lesson in a home being so much more than a structure of bricks and mortar. Living in the church parsonage taught us that our home is where we love people and show them that they have a place with us. Home is a place of belonging, rest, and peace; it is that for our own family but it can also be that for anyone who enters.

Because the church owned the house, the property, and paid the utilities (a huge blessing!!), I never really felt like the house at Hamill Road was ours anyway. It felt like we were simply stewards of a place that had been entrusted to our care for a season. Although the finishes were outdated, the bathrooms were filled with colorful tile and the back patio was often crumbling, living here was such a privilege.

During Ryan's years in seminary we were busy growing our family; welcoming three babies in four years. Having no mortgage responsibilities allowed me the blessing of staying at home or only working a very small amount of hours teaching. Looking back, that home taught me so much about contentment.

When we were finally settled into our third home, our new digs in El Paso, it felt good to have purchased our own home again. And by *purchased* I mean mortgaged and by *our own*, I mean, the Veteran's Affairs (V.A.) Loan Program. Regardless, we were happy to be in a neighborhood and have access to amenities like sidewalks throughout, wonderful neighbors, and an awesome playground and park about half a mile from our doorstep.

The lessons born in my heart on Hamill Road were continuing to grow at Redstone Pass. I was learning again that it didn't matter what your house or the furnishings inside looked like. I would realize that having an assortment of mis-matched furniture because many of our household goods had been shredded in the cross-country move, would only serve as a reminder to me. Ryan's favorite leather chair and ottoman were now covered underneath in L-brackets and carpenter's glue just to make them functional again. These mangled furnishings helped me to remember that our stuff is *just stuff*.

Redstone Pass was the perfect house for me to realize (again) that the house we inhabited was not our own. God was allowing us to be stewards of that residence much like He had done with our other homes. When God called our entire family away from our comforts and old life, I knew that He had a purpose for our entire family. Yes, Ryan was the soldier, the one whom the Army employed. However, Thomas, Mae, Kate and I were part of this ministry to the military as well. And our way of serving was by opening up the doors to our home.

Military families need and depend on one another while often being so far geographically from their own families. The way in which our family has chosen to honor God is by making our home and ourselves available to others. I believe in the deepest recesses of my heart that some of the most crucial ministry we did during our time in El Paso was done in our home. It happened when we allowed our house to be a place of generosity, of gathering, and a place of warm welcomes; no matter how humble or broken the offerings.

I hosted multiple chaplain spouse coffees, hundreds of dinner meals and play date lunches. We had birthday parties, sleepovers, and back yard tackle football at our house. We dog sat for multiple dogs, had our friends use our house as temporary lodging while we were away traveling during their Permanent Change of Station (PCS). We made gallons upon gallons of homemade ice cream to share. We entertained our next door neighbor friends on multiple occasions when they locked themselves out of their own house after school. We entertained lots of out of town family for visits and I always tried my hardest to make sure our house was an oasis of peace, rest, and comfort for them.

As much as I truly loved hosting others in my home, I enjoyed just as much serving my own family there. I consider it a joy to be able to feed my family home cooked meals around our dinner table, even if the movers scratched it. I consider it a blessing to enjoy a sunset meal on our back porch, even if we were not sitting on proper patio furniture. I consider it an act of holy service to feed others and break bread with them despite my home being far, *far* from a perfect, magazine-approved, show worthy space.

What I Needed:

I have been known to struggle with perfectionism and at times during my weaker moments, I would allow feelings of inadequacy to creep into my heart. I would look around at our belongings, an assortment of things collected, given to us, saved up for and purchased, and often I would see these things as less than or lacking.

Until recently our dining set has never been complete or fully matching. I have area rugs that belonged to other family members, many pieces of "antique" furniture that have seen better days. Ever since I have been married I have always struggled with feeling like my house and decor looked "put together." I have often said, (referring to having an "eye" for home decorating), that people either have it or they don't. And I don't have it.

And just the moment I would be ready to welcome guests, this tiny, deceptive voice would creep into my head. It would tell me that my house, my things and even my attempts were not enough. Nothing was good enough. Nothing was nice enough. Nothing was enough or worthy. I would begin to believe the lie that I needed to apologize for the things in our home.

I would sometimes openly point out the flaws in our furniture. I would often feel embarrassment about our house if I suspected the guest visiting was used to something more grandiose or elaborate. Thankfully, I was usually able to push through these negative feelings and despite them, still invite people to fellowship in our home. More times than I care to admit, I would have a pity party to Ryan and complain and belittle what we had and how it all looked. Somewhere inside of myself, I must have held a misconception that we were just not meant to have nice things.

Most of what we own inside our home is worth more of sentimental rather than material value. Honestly, you could pick up any home decor item in our home and probably find a Home Goods sticker on the bottom. I have disparaged this many times to a very patient and gently reminding husband.

What I have needed most in these moments of doubt was an assurance that God could still use me and my family in our very average, but comfortable home. I needed the reminder that as Believers we are not called to invest our treasure "*where moth or rust destroy.*" (Matthew 6:19) Our things are just things, but after our move out to El Paso, those things got pretty bruised and battered. I believed a lie that as long as Ryan was in active duty service with PCS moves every few years, there was NO hope for our household goods. We would never have nice things and if we did, they would never hold up to the

Army's contracted transportation companies. Despite my many insecurities in the overall look of our home, our scratched and dented decor, I needed a reminder that God always uses the small and broken things (and people) to do His best work. He used the widow's mite, He used the disciples' few fish and loaves of bread, and He used a woman with a small amount of precious perfume to show us what our sacrifices mean to Him.

What He Needed:

I think like most men, Ryan doesn't care so much about couch styles, large art prints or area rugs. There were many times during his work day when I would change out rugs or the placement of our kitchen furniture and he wouldn't even notice.

When I would feel like my world was ending because surely our den was too small for forty military wives to eat and fellowship in there, he would say things like, *"Don't worry about it,"* or *"You can all squeeze in."*

When I would lament that all of our worldly treasures would surely be banged up, broken, and damaged by the time the Army had moved us around a zillion times, Ryan would joke with me that I would get my mansion on streets of gold in eternity. That's typical pastor humor for you I guess.

I believe that what Ryan needed the most was to be able to come home to a house that was a place of comfort for him. I know that he always felt confident in the tidiness and coziness of our home and my ability to make a modest but flavorful meal for his work colleagues and our friends.

I also know that beyond that, Ryan put in very full days and often his work would spill over late into the night or weekends when emergencies would arise. Unfortunately this was all too often. We experienced some very tragic events during our time in the First Armored Division and as the chaplain, much of it weighed very heavily on Ryan.

Our homes should be places where at the end of a long day or shift, our soldiers may come home, take off their boots and uniform and find reprieve. Wearing the badge of honor to protect this wonderful country can often times be a heavy and difficult burden to bear.

I am not the hired help or Alice Brady of our home. I am Ryan's partner but I do want to do all I can to make our home a reprieve from his often pressure-filled, demanding work life.

Ultimately, I eventually learned to quit complaining about our belongings. It isn't Ryan's fault that the movers and transportation company have damaged our things. It certainly is not his fault that it will be probably many years before we are able to settle again anywhere permanently, therefore, avoiding broken furnishings. When I get overly grouchy about our material possessions and the ways in which they fall short, I remind myself that Ryan and I are in this thing together. We can choose to be comfortable and grateful--not always longing for more, bigger, better, or nicer.

So the best thing I can do is turn my unthankfulness into gratitude. I can be thankful for what I do have and continue to make my humble offerings to God by serving and having community with those He has placed around me. I can continue to love my neighbor as myself as I break bread and fellowship around our table and mis-matched chairs with the friends, neighbors and military community in my own back yard. In God's economy people always matter more than possessions. Relationships *always* matter more than furnishings.

From My Blog: "Letting Go of Perfectionism"

You know that classic Mary/Martha story from the Bible? The one where Martha is all a-flitter with activity trying her best to be and show her best for Jesus with all of her work? (Luke 10:38-42) And then you've got Mary (choosing the better thing) whose heart focus is on worshiping Jesus by sitting at His feet.

That story is one I think of often. If I were Martha, and let's be honest, I am Martha, I'd have been so furious with Mary. "Can't you see what all needs to be done here? Do you think this house is going to get cleaned all by itself? I could use a little help with dinner here!" Nag, nag, nag! Recently, I had a chance to choose a different path than my usual one. You see, we had company come to visit us. Ryan's mom, Becky, took a few days of her fall break to fly out to El Paso to see us.

Knowing we are having company is one thing that puts my perfectionism into overdrive. It also puts my need to plan everything and make the house, the meals, the plans, the everything...just so. For starters, Ryan and I usually give up our master bedroom and bathroom to our guests. And I try and make up a basket of goodies, gifts, chocolate, toiletries, and something to read. Becky insisted before she arrived that she wouldn't take our room, that she wanted to room with one of the kids.

We all agreed that Mae's room was best suited. With extra floor space and the bunk bed, everyone could take turns sleeping with Nana. So instead of freaking out on Mae and turning into that mean,

OCD, *it-better-pass-the-white-glove-inspection because, (gasp), what if Nana sees that you are a real kid with real toys and real messes; I simply asked Mae to clean her room. I let her know Nana would need surfaces cleared off so she could set out her things.*

I dusted, vacuumed, and put clean sheets on the bed. I also cleared a spot in the closet and gave Nana some hangers. But the rest was all Mae. It was all I could do to either put away all of these piles of stuff or at the very least tidy up these areas by folding and sorting and stacking and rearranging. And believe me, about an hour before Nana came, I almost buckled. I almost gave in to my Martha nature. I may have even been talking out loud to myself for further convincing. The letter I read myself sounded something like this:

Dear Claire,

You have a chance here to either work yourself into a tizzy and get upset that Mae's room isn't up to hotel standards. You can get a sour attitude. You can feel your blood pressure rise. You can use this last hour before your guest arrives to be busy and grumble about this mess. Or sweet self, you can let this one go. You can rest in the fact that Nana isn't coming to inspect Mae's room or judge you on how clean or neat your house is. She is coming to spend time with your family. She is coming for hugs and couch snuggles and game time and fellowship (and authentic Mexican food). So ask yourself, will obsessively clearing out all of the corners of Mae's room help accomplish any of that?

Girl, you have got to learn to chill and let some things fall away. What is the better thing here? Remember someone once told you that good enough is good enough. And sometimes the only person that cares about your best is you. Sometimes what others see and feel most is the love in your heart not the hospital corners of the sheets, or the lines in the carpet where you vacuumed or the basket of goodies or the fact that every toy is in its place.

And you know that the deeper story here is grace. It's grace for your daughter that says "I love you and appreciate your seven-and-a-half-year-old best effort at cleaning your room." It's grace for your daughter in showing her I trust her judgment on making her room look nice for Nana. It's grace for your daughter to not go behind her and redo what she has done, likely crushing her spirit. It is grace for Nana in giving her the benefit of the doubt to enjoy her time here despite some cozy, crowded corners of her accommodations. It is grace for Nana in knowing she is here for family, not here to inspect the state of the union. And it is grace for yourself to remember that your worth doesn't come from the meals you prepare or the perfections you try to procure.

So you, Claire, learn it now. Some things are best left undone, imperfect and just right as they are. In the words of one of my favorite authors, Emily P. Freeman, I "let go of the try hard life." The feeling felt good. It felt like the better thing. Yes, it did feel a little rebellious, a little out of character for me. But I'm going to be chasing this feeling more often, I can promise you that.

God's Use for the Trial:

Our Redstone Pass house was the first house that truly felt like ours after a six-year period of living in a parsonage that belonged to our church. We did have some control over choices about its location within El Paso, style of home, and other small details that mattered to us. However in many instances I failed to realize that we did NOT have control over *every* aspect of our home. And that is where the trouble lies.

Ryan and I do not use credit to make household purchases. The dilemma over how to replace or update furnishings was a difficult decision to make. Yes, the Army reimburses us a small amount for damages, but in order to replace what we really want, it takes time, savings and patience. With the military and its PCS schedule, time and patience are often luxuries we feel we cannot afford.

Ryan and I have had many conversations about whether or not to invest in nice things as long as we are serving in the Army. Even with the most careful and cautious of packers and movers, you are almost guaranteed that your property will be scratched, cracked, shredded, broken, severed, and definitely NOT in the condition that you last saw it in. Additionally, what furniture may work in your current home may not fit into your next. Or the next. Or the next. This frustration is difficult for someone who places a high importance on home and the comforts she creates there. I have always wanted roots, to feel established and to feel "at home."

Relocating to a new city, I feel this need even more urgently and intensely. I need curtains on the windows, pictures hung, and a respectable place for my family to eat meals and entertain guests. These are the things that make our house feel like a home. When you are in the military, you simply can't pass on those feelings. You can't get to living your life when it is all boxed up or broken in your garage.

When our goods came off of the truck, one of our kitchen chairs was in a dozen parts, our television console had a missing brass caster making it wobbly and uneven, Ryan's leather chair and ottoman had a broken leg each. Our son's antique desk that had belonged to Ryan's grandfather literally hit the ground as the mover backed it down the truck ramp and fell. A few of my dishes were broken and wooden footboards to one of our beds were all cracked in half.

It's just stuff. I have had to repeat this mantra to myself more times than I care to admit. *It. Is. Just. Stuff.* I know when I die, I will not take these things with me. I know the eternal perspective. I know Ryan's tired joke about my Heavenly mansion. But I live in the here and now. I am earthly and human. And I don't want broken things. I detest living with things disheveled, blemished, and bruised. Something inside me tells me that my furnishings and decor need to be perfect, and in working order. Somewhere nestled in my heart there is a metaphor in that. Maybe I have the need to feel perfect, fixed, and working just right too.

As Christians we know that apart from God, none of that is possible in our lives. God has used my furniture, my need for perfection, and my attitude toward entertaining others in our home to remind me that He uses the broken and the bruised. He makes beautiful things out of nothing. He, Himself was broken and bruised for our transgressions.

I can serve Him in my home with little or much. I can serve Him best when my attitude is one of gratitude. I can serve Him best when I am reminded that people matter *oh-so-much* more than a house of faultless beauty. My house and what is inside is not a reflection of my worth. My worth comes from my life, reborn, in Christ Jesus.

My house is where I create an environment for my husband a reprieve from his tiresome work. My house is where I teach, nurture, and disciple my children. My house is where all are welcome around our table. My house is where the Lord teaches me that true worth comes in knowing Him.

"Keep your life free from love of money (stuff, furnishings), and be content with what you have, for He has said, 'I will never leave you nor forsake you.'" {Hebrews 13:5}

A mission ready marriage understands that the people inside the home are of far more worth than the temporal things.

Questions for Reflection:

1. Which do you consider to be the "best" house you ever lived in? The "least" in the eyes of the world? For which place do you have the most special fondness? Why?

2. What are your priorities in a home? Do you prefer living in base/post in housing? Or is your preference to rent or buy a house of your choosing? What are the main factors in your decision?

3. Do you have any particular insecurities about your house or the things inside? Does this ever keep you from opening up the doors to minister to others? Why or why not?

4. Does your husband or family have any special needs that help make your home a place of peace for them? What are some of the things you do to show your love for your people that way? What would you like to do to improve in that area?

5. Is there a particular "horror story" about a beloved or irreplaceable item the transportation company broke or ruined for you? What lessons can you learn about how God may use broken and imperfect things in your life?

Chapter 5

Making 'Limonada' Out of 'Limones'

It didn't take long living in El Paso before we realized that many people stationed at Fort Bliss actually *disliked* El Paso and Fort Bliss. It felt like everywhere we turned people were knocking this place. And it was easy to believe their viewpoint if you simply took in your surroundings.

El Paso is a *unique* place. Its location is actually very remote. Yes, it is technically Texas. But practically, it is Mexico and New Mexico. The nearest large city is Albuquerque and it is a good five hour drive away. It actually takes less driving time to reach the Pacific Coast (San Diego) than it does to reach another major Texas city like Dallas or San Antonio.

Although metropolitan, El Paso is located right in the Chihuahuan Desert. There are high desert mountains that are craggy, rocky, and full of prickly vegetation. There's also a lot of dirt there. And dust. And thorns. And tumbleweeds. And a very dangerous international city minutes away. The sun and its heat are unrelenting. Outside of post, Spanish is the official language of the city. It was nearly constant that I would hear "*Como estas?*" at Target, Albertson's, and other merchants in town. El Paso is a U.S. city but it behaves in many ways like a city in Mexico.

On our drive down the main highway we traveled from our house to main post, we would pass an exit with a sign for Juarez, Mexico; a city internationally known for it's high crime, drug, and murder rates. There was a smaller sign attached bearing the message "*No Weapons*" allowed. This image did not inspire confidence or peace in my heart.

It seemed as if every military spouse I encountered was bereft of all joy at being assigned and stationed at Fort Bliss. This is ironic because it is named "Bliss," which has connotations of goodness and perfect happiness. With an already fragile heart over our new submission to the military and allowing the Army machine to set our course as a family, I panicked when all I heard was that El Paso was known as the armpit of Army locations.

Almost immediately upon arrival, I began to question God. "*Lord, why here? Why so remote? Why so far away from our families? Why so unlike what we are used to in geography, climate, lack of four seasons and culture? Lord, we are so out of our element. We are so lost here!*"

It didn't take long to realize that there was an exact purpose for our assignment to Fort Bliss. Ryan and I could see clearly that our family needed to have our first assignment fall in a place where we were solely dependent upon God for our needs and physically unable to run (or drive or fly) back quickly to the comforts of civilian life and our strong support system of our families.

I have often heard that the best way to learn a foreign language is to learn it by immersion. Move to that country, throw out your textbooks and just live among the natives. *That* is the fastest and most effective way. This was also true for us as a military family. We learned the language of the Army by immersion. Our days turned into weeks and our weeks into months. Before long, we were embracing our new home.

We made so many friends right away through the Chaplain Corps. There were chapel services, spouses' coffees, a back-to-chapel kick off picnic; there were Unit Ministry Team (UMT) potlucks, hails and farewells. One of my first stops was the Protestant Women of the Chapel (PWOC) kickoff where I immediately signed up for a weekly Bible study.

In our neighborhood, we met so many nice families. The day our household goods arrived, a sweet neighbor, Lucy, a few doors down, welcomed us with a plate full of homemade treats. My awesome new friend, Samantha, across the street brought us a homemade dinner. Only a few short months later I would discover, down the street from my doorstep, my *best* El Paso friend, Cathy who is also a chaplain's wife and fellow homeschooling mom. Her kids became like siblings to ours.

We began to explore activities for our kids. We all fell in love with a wonderful golf program, The First Tee of Greater El Paso, and spent nearly every Tuesday with some of the best coaches and mentors anyone could ever ask for. We found friends at the local First Baptist church where our kids participated in Upward basketball and cheerleading during the deployment, and where Ryan and I participated in Financial Peace University.

I still remember one baseball season when our son Thomas, then nine, played for a local baseball team. He was literally the only non-Hispanic player on the team. This was our first foray into *local* El Paso team sports. At team sign-ups in Chattanooga, we had been used to getting a pair of gray pants at a sporting goods store and having a screen printed t-shirt for the team uniform.

The uniforms in El Paso were hand stitched and lettered in Mexico and resembled the quality of those worn by professional athletes. There was a team of seamstresses that came from Juarez to take measurements of each player in order to custom fit his uniform. El Pasoans take their *'beisbol'* seriously.

Additionally, all of the siblings and parents were expected to order coordinating t-shirts to wear to the baseball games letting everyone know that she was "*Mother of #22*" or "*Sister of #22*." Throughout the entire season, every player's mother would give huge hugs and little air kisses on each cheek to one other. Every mother. Every game. Can you guess how many kisses I got? If you guessed zero or none you would be correct. I was on the outside of their customs and culture.

At every game there was a local food truck that refrained from selling popcorn or peanuts. Instead they offered '*chicharrones de harina*' (fried Mexican pork crisps in the shape of a wagon wheel) and '*elotes*' (grilled corn on the cob). To wash all of that down you might indulge in an '*aguas frescas*' (fresh fruit waters).

During that same season, Ryan was away for several weeks on a pre-deployment field exercise and I had agreed to host a spouses' coffee at our house. This event fell on a night that Thomas had a baseball game and I just figured he would have to miss and stay with his sisters and his babysitter. Thomas's coach, Sal, had a different idea in mind. He graciously offered to come by our house to pick Thomas up and bring him home because he needed his star third baseman. I hesitantly agreed. I didn't really know this man but I knew Thomas wanted to play in his game.

The night of the coffee I was surely busy with preparations and making food, arranging flowers, and rehearsing my devotion to share. But in a moment of clarity I found myself chuckling. We had been in a new city for less than a year. Ryan was gone and here I was letting practically a stranger whose last name I barely knew come pick up my son, the only non-native Spanish speaker on his team and drive him to ball fields within walking distance to the United States/Mexico border at Cuidad Juarez.

In our former, civilian life, there would have been NO WAY we would have EVER allowed this. If Ryan or I had been unable to get one of our children to an activity we had a grandparent or family member list about eight deep we could rely on in a pinch. At the time, in El Paso there were about three people I knew and trusted well enough to shuttle my kids somewhere, and two of those three women would be attending the coffee at my house.

It was in this moment that I realized some valuable truths. I realized that it does, indeed, take a village to raise kids. And sometimes we just have to realize that the dynamics of our villages change. We had been in a village primarily composed of loving family members and people who looked and spoke just like us. Living in El Paso showed me that our village may look or sound a little different and that can be celebrated.

None of us can do it all on our own; especially when our husbands are frequently out of town and we are needing extra sets of hands and wheels to get our kids where they need to be. These are some of God's greatest graces to us.

During another outing when Ryan was away, I laughed when we attended a friend's birthday party at Bob-O's, one of those huge outdoor play places. My daughter, Mae, then seven, had desperately wanted to ride Go-Carts. Due to her size she was required to have an adult ride along. I have three children and there's only one of me. So she needed a driver.

I have a picture someone took of Mae smiling joyously, riding shotgun with a random Bob-O's employee driving her around that track like crazy. In this military life, there are often times we have to have stand-ins for dad. I like to call these *Pseudo-Padres* or *Deployment Daddies*. And *that*, too, can be celebrated. It DOES take a village. These are stand-ins, not replacements.

Whether you are in the desert of El Paso, stationed in Germany, Korea, or in the deep South, people are people and people are mostly good. Our accents and dialects may differ, be we are all the same. You say '*limon*,' I say '*lemon*.'

Our family was especially thankful for the military community and the activities and amenities on post, but we were also grateful for our varied multicultural experiences off post. The local baseball experience was only the tip of the iceberg. There were many days that we felt like the outcasts, underdogs, and outnumbered misfits that we were. God can sometimes teach us the most when we feel the most uncomfortable.

What I Needed:

It seems to me that what I needed was exactly what I got.
I needed to move away from the familiar to learn this lesson.
There is no doubt in my mind that had we lived anywhere
near our homes and families in Tennessee we would have
continued to find ways to rely on their physical help and
hands.

Whether it was coaches or theme park workers or other
dads or mom friends, it takes all hands on deck many days to
survive. I sure didn't want to see my kids miss out on normal
parts of childhood all because Dad's duty calls and takes him
away from home on many occasions. So the alternative is to
set aside your pride and your attitude that you, in fact, can do
it all yourself (because there is logistically NO WAY you can)
and invite others in your community into the process.

I needed to realize that Thomas's coach and many others
around us really are placed in our path to help us carry the
load, to help ease our burdens. I quickly realized that people
(both civilian and military) are very grateful and sensitive to
the specialized needs of military families. I needed to be
reminded above all that God has our best interests in His
hands. Those baseball moms may not have showered me with
their love, but God does! He is gracious to provide us what

we need, when we need it and that often comes in the form of *who* we need.

Rides to practice, basketball or golf coaches, neighbors offering to pull weeds, a Christian family camp inviting you to attend while your husband is away, or another chaplain's family helping with drop offs and pickups at the airport… needing help in these situations is not the end of the world. In fact, they are huge blessings in disguise. These are ways the Lord says, "*Here's a small glitch* (lemon) *in your plans...and here's how/who I am providing for you so that you can enjoy life nonetheless* (lemonade)."

Or maybe I should say '*aguas frescas con limon.*'

What He Needed:

Thankfully Ryan is not a jealous person or one who is suspicious of the goodwill in others. Ryan has shown much gratitude for the help others have provided when he has been away or unable to be counted on as a partner in our parenting. When he signed on the dotted line, I feel sure that Ryan did not wholly understand the full measure of the commitment his military service would require.

He knew his unit would be busy but even he could never have known how much he would be away during this first duty assignment. I believe that it gave him much peace of mind to know that our kids were not missing out on too much in terms of their extra-curricular and enrichment activities. His absence didn't require their sitting out on fun.

It helped him to know that by allowing and agreeing to help when we needed it, my own stress level was lower. I think it even assuaged some of his guilt of being away knowing that there were other fill-ins and hands to help run the show.

I think Ryan's temperament helped immensely in this situation. Ryan is easy-going. And although typically an "*I don't need any help*" kind of guy, while he was away he absolutely invited the help for his family. Ryan did not feel too proud, arrogant, or over-bearing to impose our minimal needs for assistance on others. That was just the way it was and had to be. Might as well get over it and accept the help.

This is yet another way in which Ryan was able to stay mission ready while he was at training and during the deployment. In a way, me having reasonable help allowed him to be worry-free about things at the 'hacienda' while he was helping to protect the freedoms of our country.

And as far as El Paso is concerned, Ryan, too became very fond of the Mexican culture and to this day rates his affinity for Casa de Torta's pork cubana and L&J's tampiquena steak as two of his favorite meals anywhere. The views and beauty of the trails in the Franklin Mountains are some of the most breathtaking we have ever seen. Watching the minor league, El Paso Chihuahuas baseball team at Southwest University Park holds many fond memories for our family. Life in a new place is what you make it. We have declared that our family mantra will be to embrace where we are and enjoy the unique aspects of every assignment. It will be time to leave the very place that has grown so dear to you even before you know it!

From My Blog: "Some Thoughts on El Paso and Why Fort Bliss is the Best Kept Secret in the Army"

When I think about the time we have been here at Fort Bliss, way out here in El Paso, Texas I know that I will forever remember it as a place where God provided! I admit, I don't always recognize and acknowledge that provision in the moment. Ryan often tells me I am a pessimist and a Chicken Little. And in the moment I'd have to agree that he is right. I am bad to look at the present and see what's wrong, or what's missing, or the challenges of the immediate. I am also bad to look into the future and think of all of the "What ifs?" the "Hows?" and the "Whys?"

However, give me a rear-view mirror and I can see forever into the beauty and blessings of where I have been and Who has shown me His loving mercy. When I take the time to look back and reflect, I can totally see Him at work in my days. Those moments when there's only one set of footprints in the sand...well there were a lot of moments over these past few years when God has carried me.

Right here, in this place of isolation, dusty brown windstorms, and thorns...He has carried me! Today I am imagining that someone asked me what is so great about El Paso and what makes Fort Bliss such a special place?

On a basic, practical or logistic level El Paso is a nice big city. There are tons and tons of things to do here. We have seen plays, gone to *countless museums, been to see baseball games, eaten some of the BEST Mexican food of our lives. We have had access to all of the amenities of a big city: multiple Target stores, TJ Maxx and Marshall's. (Give me a Target and a TJ and I can be as happy as a lark!) There's a great whole foods store on the west side of town, Sprouts. We have been to the zoo a bunch, we have ice skated and we have seen the SuperCroc.*

On post, there is just about everything you need and more. Fort Bliss has an outstanding commissary, an oh-so-fun Freedom Crossing with tons of dining and entertainment options. There's bowling, tennis, and wonderful chapels on post. There's a fantastic library, reliable childcare, great Child and Youth Services (CYS) and Morale, Welfare and Recreation (MWR) programs. We have done music lessons, tennis lessons, story time, and the homeschool PE class.

Near here, we have made many fun excursions to Ruidoso, New Mexico, to Cloudcroft, to the New Mexico Museum of Space History, to White Sands National Monument, Hueco Tanks, to Carlsbad Caverns and to Albuquerque, New Mexico. One day I even (accidentally) ventured onto the International Bridge to try and get a peek at Juarez, Mexico. We have taken part in the Day of the Cowboy, Kidsapalooza and we have seen local artists. Shall I go on?

We have hunted Easter eggs. We have Trick-or-Treated. We have Trunk-or-Treated. We have learned the fine art of tamale making. We rang bells for the Salvation Army. We have Walked/Run to Remember.

We have joined the YMCA. We have played on the baseball team, the local football team and we have been gymnasts and cheerleaders. We have enjoyed the blessings of the Upward program at FBC. We have performed in "The Star Factor" and the "Fumbly Bumbly Angels." We have played golf, golf, and more golf. We have enjoyed spouses' coffees with chaplains and unit friends. We have had visitors and more visitors. We have learned the art of cooking all of the Thanksgiving food. We have been Baptized. We have finished marathons and half-marathons. We have eaten off of the food truck that comes through our neighborhood.

We have ventured to the beaches of Coranado and San Diego. Twice. We have seen the Grand Canyon. We have enjoyed the heck out of our neighborhood park. We have celebrated birthday after birthday after birthday. Some with friends. Some just family. We have been neighborly. And we have had to adjust and readjust the calendar. We have homeschooled. We have entertained guests. We have made cookies. We have survived our first deployment. We have presided. And we have flourished.

When I look back and think back on just what all we have done here I will be terribly sad to leave this wonderful place. But I would be remiss if I didn't address what has made all of this greatness possible. You see what has made this season at Fort Bliss so memorable, so wonderful has been the PEOPLE.

The people we have encountered have made this experience so rich and beautiful. I won't name specific names because there are too many to

*count. I have encountered some of the most selfless, giving, humble,
service-minded folks since the day we arrived at Fort Bliss. We have had
instant friends who have cooked us meals and met us for lunch. Shown
us the ropes. Given us a listening ear. Given us wisdom and
encouragement. Shown us care and concern.*

*From off-post churches who care, to realtors, doctors, coaches and
hair-stylists...all of the good people have just found their way to us.
Seriously, the kindness of the people of El Paso, of Fort Bliss and of
the Army have been nothing shy of gems. The thing about these people is
that I don't think their kindness and goodness is exclusive to El Paso or
Fort Bliss. I think this kindness and goodness truly exists in many
people, in many places. I think it's everywhere. We just have to look for
it.*

*There are no secrets, no magic formulas for happiness or making a
place home. The truth of the matter is simple. Many days it feels as if
my heart is so small and fragile. Many days it feels as though my heart
lacks the courage and strength to make one more transition; to settle into
one more new set of circumstances. Many days I worry that I don't have
the emotional energy to say one more hello or one more tearful goodbye or
"see you later." Just when you think your heart can't stand anymore
stretching or pulling you take a deep breath, steel yourself, dig-down-deep
and realize that your heart isn't really so small or tiny or weak. Your
heart isn't fragile or broken.*

You realize your heart is actually steadfast. It is full. It is actually a giant, happy heart. It's happy because Christ makes His home there. But it is also happy because it is brimming with the abundance of the good life you have. It is abounding in the reassurance that though at times we feel the pains of sadness, the prick of worry, the stabs of despair, at the end of the day there is a deep-seated joy.

Maybe I'm the only one. Maybe I'm just SUPER in touch with my emotions. But I told Ryan the other night that being an Army (military) spouse is sometimes like trudging through quick sand. All you really want to do is stand up and stand firm. But it feels like every. single. time. you start to get your footing, you lose it again. Every time you start to develop deep friendships, it's time for someone to move. Every time it feels like your marriage is in a great place, your solider leaves for another drill, training, time in the field, a trip TDY or worst of all, a deployment. Every time you have gotten accustomed to yet, another, new normal…guess what? Time for another change!

Throughout our time in the Army (be it long or short) I know I am going to have to continue adapting. I'm going to have to continue to slog through the quick sand of being a military spouse. I am going to have to continue to show resilience. I want to grow in wisdom. I want to grow in my faith. I want my already full and abundant heart to have room for more friends, more relationships, more testing, more growing, and ultimately more strength.

Maybe you have shared similar struggles as one who resists change. Maybe, like me, you shy away from the hard stuff. Maybe, like me, you find yourself constantly at a heart crossroads. Be encouraged. You are right where God wants you! You are right where He can speak to you, and use you and ultimately love you! You see, He has shown me that He wanted me here, in El Paso, at Fort Bliss. He has spoken to me here, He has used me here. And He has LOVED me here!

God's Use for the Trial:

Since I was young I have always had an independent spirit. I have always held a deeply (albeit falsely) rooted belief that "*I can do it myself.*" I just have one of those personalities that absolutely despises asking for or receiving any help. Somewhere inside of me I have believed that this need for others' intervention is a sign of weakness or imposition. I hate to bother other people with what I perceive are my problems or my own needs.

What God showed me through our time way out in El Paso was that I surely could *not* do it all on my own. I could not even count on being able to do it on *our* own as a family when Ryan would be away over 50% of our time there. I realized quickly that Ryan was off the list of possible help when he was in the field, at the National Training Center (NTC) or at Camp Nathan Smith.

The certain hiccups that we all experience in life like flat tires, needing to be two or three places at one time or even just feeling frazzled, can be met with more frustration and a crippling inability to act. Or with the Lord's help, we can invite Him into our situations and see that He has placed other willing kingdom workers all around us. When I put the weight of having all of life's problems solved by Ryan on *Ryan's shoulders*, it's too much weight for our marriage to often bear. But when I exchange those burdens with the Lord and rest in His provision, the marriage relationship stays aligned and balanced. These folks can show up in unexpected places and in unexpected ways, but when they do, you just know they were divinely appointed to be at the right place at the right time.

I pray that my eyes and heart are always sensitive to these times when God smiles at us and reminds us of His omniscience and presence in the details of our lives. I also pray that as I see others in need and cross paths with other military spouses in situations where they may need a hand, that I am the first to offer mine!

"And let us consider how to stir up one another to love and do works, not neglecting to meet together, as is the habit of some, but encouraging one another..." {Hebrews 10:24-25}

A mission ready marriage appreciates that God places us where He wants us in each season.

Questions for Reflection:

1. Have you ever been stationed somewhere where nearly everyone you encountered had a negative reaction to your new place? Where was it and how did you handle this negativity?

2. Did you ever feel like you didn't fit into the "norms" of your military or civilian community? What made you feel like an outcast? How did you break in and find a place for yourself or family? What kind of personal or spiritual growth came about as a result of your willingness to join in? Like my hurt feelings with not being the object of the baseball moms' affections, was there a time when you had to immerse and yet you still felt out of the loop?

3. Have you ever had to rely on others during a time when your service member was away? See how many instances you can think of. Which was the most ridiculous or humorous?

4. How has this type of "*it takes a village*" mentality affected your marriage? Have you or your spouse had any malice toward each other because of this? Have there been any jealous feelings? How have you dealt with these challenges?

Can your marriage truly be mission ready when there's resentment at play?

5. How have you seen God working in you during times when you felt that you had to "make lemonade out of lemons?" Describe what made this experience bittersweet. Did you ever get to a point where there was more sweetness than bitterness?

Chapter 6

Preparing to Say Goodbye

As soon as Ryan received his official orders to Fort Bliss and his assignment to the First Armored Division, we knew right away that being part of a combat brigade meant one thing: combat. Although, I think we had this hunch long before the Army made it official.

My husband, a regular GI Joe, had actually *volunteered* to list a combat unit on his preference sheet. Despite being a non-combatant, my chaplain had no desire to be locked away in an office drowning in paperwork and Power Point presentations. He wanted to be on the front lines and in on the action. The Lord and the Army heard his prayers and willingly obliged.

With Operation Enduring Freedom (OEF) well underway, we realized that it would be only a matter of time before Ryan and his brothers and sisters in arms would be heading downrange to Afghanistan. They were slated for deployment by the end of 2012. We had heard the deployment would last twelve months. Then we heard nine months with possible extensions. We had also heard rumors the entire deployment may only last six months. If you have spent five minutes in the military, you know firsthand that often information and details are as clear as mud.

We arrived in El Paso in late August of 2011. By February of 2012 Ryan's unit was performing regular field exercises and rigorous training. By August of 2012, he left for a month-long training to the National Training Center (NTC) at Fort Irwin, California. As the days drew nearer, Ryan felt more mission ready than ever. I, on the other hand, began to seriously question and doubt (again) that God had the right family in mind for what He was about to call us to do.

During the pre-deployment there is the strangest tension in the air. The soldier (in this case, Ryan), is trained and ready. He or she is literally chomping at the bit to get this thing underway. Essentially, the past year of training and readiness preparations are finally able to be put into practice and put to use. However there is also a mounting sadness at the impending separation from family and loved ones.

As the spouse, I, too, felt my share of tension. I was absolutely devastated to think about Ryan being gone from us for the greater part of 2013. There were days when I was so sad, tearful, and upset I didn't think I was going to be able to drive him to his drop off the morning of his report date.

I was worried about the effects of his separation on our children who had already been having sentimental, emotional moments in the weeks leading up. I was especially worried about the damage such a long physical separation might do to our marriage. It was strong already, but was it *Army Strong?*

Like all things military related, whether I wanted Ryan to go to Afghanistan or not was a moot point. He had orders from the President of the United States. It was a done deal. He was going and this I knew for sure. So another part of my divided heart was just ready for him to leave already. I had begun mentally preparing for self-reliance and autonomy.

The mounting emotional pressures and sadness was almost palatable in the final weeks. Every "*I love you*" meant so much more. Every hug, kiss, or embrace felt like it might as well be the last. Despite the statistics of safety and low numbers for actual life-threatening danger being on my side, when you send your loved one into harms way amidst a war-zone, you can't help but let troubling thoughts build up in your mind. All of the potential tragic scenarios can't help but fester there; statistics be darned.

We had to prepare legal documents like our living wills and powers of attorney before Ryan could exit the country. We had a file of all of our important documents in one convenient location *just in case*. And the final blow to my fragile psyche came the night I decided to attend the Care Team training just weeks before Ryan left.

I had already received my Level I, II, and III Army Family Team Building (AFTB) training and certificates. I had also done an online version of the Family Readiness Group

(FRG) training. But going to the Care Team training live and in person made our deployment a little too real for me.

I was reminded of the casualty notification process. I was briefed on the role of both the FRG and the Care Team during this process. Food handling and chain of command instructions were given. Resources for Gold Star families were discussed. Service Member's General Life Insurance (SGLI) disbursements along with funeral and memorial service arrangements were highlighted.

After receiving my certificate, I drove myself home and emailed our Headquarters (HHT) FRG team lead and asked her to kindly remove my name from the Care Team roster for our squadron. I knew I didn't possess the stoicism or resolution to help in that way. I was selfishly envisioning myself in the role of a young widow and how our life would be dramatically and drastically altered and it all hit too close to home, too soon before I was sending my Ryan off to war.

I was able to stay on as a Key Caller and make monthly phone calls to soldiers' parents, spouses and/or next of kin with friendly updates about our unit, but I felt that was all I could contribute. In this exact moment, my own selfishness and fear far outweighed my call to service.

Ryan and I would spend the days in December of 2012 finding the balance between going through the rituals and liturgy of the everyday and our certain depressing reality. We would try to push away the thoughts of what was to come. We had plenty of quality family time and a few date nights. I had a sense of dread in my heart that impatiently said, "*Please, just go already.*" We were each one anxious to get the deployment underway so that we could be one day closer to having it over!

What I Needed:

It became clear to me that the brunt of my worries surrounded security. I needed promises that Ryan would not purposely volunteer for potentially dangerous missions that were non-essential for the chaplain to be part of. I needed the security of knowing that he would find a way whenever and wherever possible to stay in touch through email, FaceTime and occasional phone calls and text messages from a disposable, international cell phone.

I needed the security of knowing that we had our legal and financial business in order. If the worst were to happen, I needed a tangible, realistic plan of action. As painful and cryptic as it felt and seemed at the time, I needed to be able to articulate and address these issues with Ryan face to face before he left. I had all of our essential documents and account passwords at my fingertips.

I needed to feel the promise and stability of knowing I had an emergency plan in place in town, in El Paso. It would have taken two days of driving or at a minimum a six hour flight, for any of our family members to reach us. Ryan and I made a plan with our neighbors, and two close chaplain families (one who was deploying with Ryan and one who was staying in El Paso) to be our points of contact should I have an emergency and need the help of another adult.

We took the time and money and invested in setting up service for a reliable home security system. I wasn't afraid to be at our house alone, but it gave me great comfort to know when we traveled or were away, that our house would be securely protected. There is just something about a sign in the yard, stickers and alarms on the windows that promised the hope of a deterrent towards burglary.

I also came to rely heavily on other friends in our unit and acquaintances from PWOC who were also facing deployment. There's truth in the statement that there's *"strength in numbers."* For whatever reason, I felt through the bonds of Army wife-dom and sisterhood, that going through a deployment with literally hundreds of my acquaintances I would be okay. I knew I was not alone and I knew others were walking the painful road too.

I needed the confidence to know that although the deployment and lengthy separation would be tiresome and difficult, I had assurance to know beyond a shadow of a doubt that I could handle it. I would survive.

What He Needed:

Ironically enough, I think Ryan ended up needing many of the same things I needed. He needed a guarantee and encouragement that the kids and I would be okay. It calmed him to know that legally, financially, and practically our needs would be mostly met.

Another area where Ryan felt strongly was that of the relational aspects of the separation. Of course, I would miss him and experience the loneliest season of our marriage to date, but staying in El Paso, I would have Thomas, Mae and Kate constantly with me. I would have their physical touches and their needs to care for to keep my days full and my heart rejoicing. I would also have the benefit of our neighborhood, chapel, off-post church, PWOC, homeschool community, kids' sports and unit fellowship to interact and engage with.

Ryan would basically be in a small officer's barracks in a three room suite attached to the chapel at Camp Nathan Smith in Kandahar City. He was also considering our communication and ways to keep our relationship and marriage intact.

Several weeks before he left, we had a brainstorming session where we each gave some suggestions of ways to stay in touch. We also decided what kinds of messages and information would be helpful and not so helpful to share with one another during this unique time. He agreed that he needed me to keep him informed of what was going on at a basic, need-to-know-information level. He knew it would be difficult on him for me to constantly give too many details about problems with the kids or with the house. Ryan is a fixer and when he was half a world away, there was no physical way possible he could help fix anything. Having to hear too much about it would only stress him out.

We also knew that his time for communication would be irregular and often interrupted. Therefore we knew it would be crucial to start and end our conversations with some highlights and not just the bad news or complaints. When you know that each time you are communicating with your soldier could be your last, you want to make sure each conversation is seasoned with kindness and grace.

Ryan and I continued to collaborate on ideas and goals we could work toward together despite our distance. I got him professional stationery printed up and he mailed me a letter each week and mailed each of our three kids a letter each week as well. I planned monthly themed care packages to send. We agreed to watch as many Oscar winning movies as possible and attempted to read a few of the same books. We made it a priority to have some "us" things to talk about and focus upon even though the War on Terror was the proverbial white elephant in the room.

From My Blog: "Just Fine"

It has been a while since I've really spent any time with a real post with words and thoughts here in this space. I can't even describe how busy things have been around here but trust me, we are all five going on all cylinders. I know once Ryan gets gone things are going to slow down to a snail's pace but for now these weeks and days are zooming by. So what have we really been up to?

Ryan leaves sometime during the second or third week of December. He's been super busy at work with all manner of things. They have started packing up their personal belongings and gear to ship over to Afghanistan. Seeing his individual first aid kit and his blood type taped to his Kevlar has been a real reminder of the possible danger I am sending my husband into.

There's been a certain sense of angst in the air with Ryan leaving soon. Nothing major or bad. I think it's just normal. Although we don't relish this separation I think we are both just ready to get on with it. I'm not sure that makes sense to a lot of people but there are so many physical and emotional preparations we are all making and the tension of it all is building. We are talking about things with the kids more and more and trying to live normally and yet trying to prepare them (and ourselves) for (another) new transition.

In related news and in full disclosure, I have had some twinges of my old friend, anxiety, creeping in. I stopped taking Zoloft prescribed by my OB-GYN, back in July (gradually) and by early August I was off of it completely. I just didn't like how it was making me feel (insatiably hungry). Having said that, I worry (how ironic?) that maybe I should be on medication again in order to get through this deployment.

I went to my primary-care doctor for a checkup a few weeks ago and just let him know that I had come off of this medication. I was essentially seeking his blessing in doing so. I shared with him my history of postpartum depression, seeing a counselor, a short-term use of Lexapro to bump my chemicals/hormones back into place and then most recently by use of the Zoloft back in February of this year. It's a slippery slope with these medications. I know I have some crazy hormonal and physical issues going on but I also know that some of how I feel is often situational. Right now a deployment feels like a situation alright!

This doctor was very patient with me sharing my medical history and he basically told me that I would be "Just Fine" during this deployment. He asked a series of questions about the kids, my family, friends here, a support system, stress-coping mechanisms. His conclusion? Yes, I will feel stressed and worried and tired some times. But that is normal and to be expected.

All I pretty much need is the medical stamp of approval from a doctor to tell me I am normal and healthy and that sets my heart and mind at ease. Anyway, the verdict is that we will all be fine. I'll be fine. It will all be fine. I really am thankful that despite busyness and some big family changes the Lord is faithful to supply me with much peace and patience these days. He is good. His Word is true and I know He walks with me every day.

God's Use for the Trial:

On multiple occasions Ryan and I have fondly reflected upon those final weeks leading up to his departure. We agree that it was by far, one of the most bittersweet times of our entire marriage. I would liken it to throwing yourself off of a cliff. In order to go through with it, you know you have to walk up to the edge. You know the free-fall is coming, but you just can't make yourself take steps toward the edge. It is a weird situation full of countless emotions.

The sweet part of this time was Ryan and I really and truly came to a defining moment in our marriage that will forever stand as a beautiful crossroads for us. All of our feelings and emotions were reduced to a real life testing of our marriage vows. Did we mean what we proclaimed at the altar?

All of the inconsequential, minute, and petty arguments cease. All of the hard feelings and grievances melt away. Every moment we have together feels treasured and special. All of the moments and years of taking one another for granted feel like a big mistake. Suddenly you realize what you have in your spouse. You appreciate your marriage as perfectly imperfect with all of its flaws, warts, and blemishes. We bonded in a unique way and held tightly to what we had in each other.

And I know God was in the midst of our renewed commitment from the moment He called us to this military ministry until the moment Ryan landed back, safely in El Paso nine months later. God's design for marriage is and has always been the act of two individual people coming together in Him, with mutual submission for each other. And through our pre-deployment phase Ryan and I finally began to see our promises to one another as a means for solidarity and unity. The personal pain and long-suffering we were about to endure would stretch us to our limits of personal (and missional) devotion and faithfulness. We clung to one another in a way unlike any other. We trusted that our faith in God and our faith in our marriage would anchor and sustain us.

"Though one may be overpowered, two can defend themselves. A cord of three strands is not quickly broken." {Ecclesiastes 4:12}

A mission ready marriage asserts that "We are in this together even when we are apart."

Questions for Reflection:

1. During your years in military service, has your spouse had to deploy? How many times? What was his level of personal danger?

2. Did the time leading up to the deployment affect your marriage? Did it make you bitter or better? Do you tend to pull away? Fall to pieces? Cling tightly? What did you both do to become more mission ready as a couple and as individuals?

3. What are some practical ways you and your spouse choose to stay connected, close, and intimate during the separation? Do those strategies work? Why or why not?

4. Does your marriage feel like a partnership? What do you feel are your greatest strengths you bring to the relationship? What are your spouse's? How can you accentuate each other's strengths?

5. Like my episode of panic with my doctor, was there ever a time leading up to a deployment or extended separation that you struggled with excessive worry or whether or not you would survive or be "okay?"

Chapter 7

Thriving Through a Deployment

For all of the months of tension and stress that led up to
Ryan's departure, once he left I had a nearly instant feeling of
resolve. It was as if a mental switch flipped and I got into
"Let's do this" mode. The morning we dropped Ryan off at his
squadron headquarters, I took the kids to breakfast, and then
we went to our chapel service just like we normally would
have. I fought back a few tears but largely the kids and I held
up well.

The next day when we woke up it was Christmas Eve.
Although we had celebrated a mock Christmas Eve and
Christmas Day before Ryan left, the kids and I stayed around
the house packing for our Tennessee trip the following day.
That evening, I made a homemade chicken-pot-pie and set
the table with linens and candles. After picking at our food,
we piled into our vehicle and drove to a special Christmas
Eve service on the installation.

It seemed that despite my fears and worries about how
this would go, we were going to make it. The sun would rise
and set each day, we would mark the days and months on our
calendars and before we knew it Ryan and Daddy would be
back in our arms.

In the time leading up to our deployment, I had heard many, many wives joke about something called the "Deployment Curse." This was a new term to me, and much like the expression, "Army Brat," it did not bear a positive connotation. Furthermore, I don't believe in curses. When friends and more seasoned wives would speak of this curse, I simply did not believe them. In fact, it sounded downright silly and I for one was *not* going to give any credence or claim to something that sounded like hogwash.

I didn't believe it until the second day of the deployment, Christmas Day, when a freak ice storm hit the Dallas/Fort Worth airport, thereby shutting down all flights in and out of the place. Thomas, Mae, Kate and I were only supposed to have a 55 minute layover and then be in route to Chattanooga in time for Christmas dinner. But that one hour eventually turned into twelve. My kids slept under airport benches that night. I made friends with a mom and daughter who were on our original flight and would later also be returning to the Chattanooga airport to hunt down our lost luggage. By some miracle we finally got re-routed to Atlanta where my dad graciously picked us up at 4:00 am and drove us the two hours north to Chattanooga. After being awake for over 24 straight hours, I began to wonder if that Deployment Curse might actually exist.

We spent a lovely two weeks with my family and Ryan's and I felt brave and settled. If nothing else, I felt distracted from our reality. I had some contact with Ryan; he had arrived in country and had made his way safely to his quarters. I was relieved he had arrived without delay or incident. We flew back to El Paso (uneventfully, thank goodness) and really got our end of the deployment underway.

After being back home for only a few days all of our smoke detector batteries began beeping intermittently. There were seven in all, and four of them were upstairs in the eaves of our vaulted ceilings. I had to get out Ryan's ladder and extend it as far as it would slide. I climbed up to the very highest rung to reach the detectors. I did this seven times on a very wobbly ladder with my nine-year-old son spotting me at the bottom.

A few weeks after that, my oldest daughter, Mae complained of her tummy hurting on our drive home from Upward basketball and cheer practice. Moments later she vomited inside our van all over the carpet floorboards and herself. This night marked a nine day streak where all four of us passed around a violent stomach bug. One person would present symptoms for a day or two and clear up only to have them reappear a day or two later. There were fevers, aches, and more coming out both ends than I care to remember. I was scrubbing carpets, hosing off rugs in my driveway, scouring toilets and showers, and doing loads of bedding in my washer and dryer like a mad woman. And I did all of this while I, too, was battling the stomach virus. We did not leave the house for nine days and were it not for my neighbor bringing Gatorade and Lysol, we may have never emerged. I may have cried once, or a dozen times, during that week.

It was during the midst of this plague that I remember feeling very mad at Ryan. He would FaceTime us after he'd had a refreshing two hour workout at the gym and was eating a hot breakfast of eggs, oatmeal, juice, and coffee. He looked so chipper, well rested, and energized on that computer screen; deployment was agreeing with him. I resented the HECK out of him not being at home with us to help take part in caring for our sick children and me. While we were lacking energy and surviving on dry toast, I may have secretly wished Ryan could somehow catch our virus through the Internet waves.

Over the next several months, I would tackle all of my normal mother/wife duties of schooling the children, cleaning, cooking, serving as President of the Fort Bliss PWOC chapter, caring for boo-boos, wiping tears, giving extra hugs, and having extra bed buddies in the middle of the night when the kids were especially missing Dad.

In addition, I was keeping our cars serviced and in working order, negotiating new tires for my vehicle, keeping our yard watered and mowed, repairing belts on my vacuum cleaner, replacing a broken deadbolt on our front door, and learning the art of watching a YouTube video to take apart my dryer to replace and clean out the internal lint screen. I was monitoring our bank accounts, keeping bills paid, and planning periodic trips and treats for the kids to keep us busy. We would also experience our one and only ER visit during the time Ryan was gone. It turns out that an appendicitis attack presents the same symptoms as severe constipation. Who knew? Yes, Deployment Curse indeed!

During those months, our kids continued their weekly golf lessons, started and finished a basketball/cheer season, took music lessons, attended weekly Bible studies and chapel services. We entertained several sets of family visitors, and had friends over regularly for dinners and play dates. We celebrated holidays and special occasions like celebrities. We were busy little bees, and although tiring and exhausting on me at times, looking back I wouldn't have done things any differently.

What I Needed:

While it seems like our deployment experience could be reduced to a few clever paragraphs with many of the high and low points connected with many commas, that really was not the case at all. There were days that felt like months; weeks that felt like years. There were many, many moments of unbearable loneliness, anxiety, exhaustion, frustration with Ryan, with the Army and with our circumstances.

About two thirds of the way through, our brigade experienced the heartbreak of several casualties. One of my PWOC sisters received the dreaded knock on her door that no spouse ever wants to get. During periods when there were enforced "no communication" mandates and no contact from our soldiers, everyone was on edge in a realistic panic. Our dear sister and her two young children were now living their worst nightmare. We cried with her, ached in the deepest corners of our hearts for her and for her children.

It was a new emotion for me to feel such a mixture of grief and sadness but also feel relief and joy in the same moment. I was distraught for my friend. I was grieving for her in a way I had never known. I wanted to reach out to care for her, to help her. I offered to watch her children, I took her meals. I made her a CD of some worship music.

And in my small ways I tried to minister to her in the only, feeble way I knew how. I suddenly remembered a phrase I had uttered to Ryan while he was at CH-BOLC. *"How in the heck would making a casserole or offering to clean her house make one iota of difference in a situation like that?"* It turns out, just showing up and being present to care is about all anyone can do.

As much as I grieved for my friend, at the VERY same time, I felt such relief and joy that it was not my door that received a knock for casualty notification. I felt such respite and a release of fear and anxiety that it was not my soldier, my Ryan, that was deceased. It wasn't Thomas, Mae, and Kate's daddy that would be sent back to the U.S. in a flag-draped casket. For that I was extremely grateful and comforted.

I really didn't know what to do with those feelings. From that moment on, the tenor and vibe of the whole deployment took on a new twist. I felt guilt and gratitude. I felt sadness and relief. But after our brigade's first casualties, my worries and fears for Ryan's safety reached new heights. I needed to daily reframe my thoughts and keep my prayer life vigilant. I needed to cultivate a daily practice of keeping a gratitude list. I needed to surround myself with other spouses walking this road. Often we needed to weep together and shoulder one another's grief for our dear, sweet sister.

I needed to believe Ryan was coming home whole and healthy at the end of the deployment despite the fact that he, nor the Army, or even God could offer me any guarantees. I needed faith more than ever.

What He Needed:

Ryan has actually told me that the thing he needed most leading up to the deployment and during his time away was an unspoken blessing from me. He needed me to know that he did *not* want to go away to war. He did not want to be away from us; but as a man, soldier and patriot, it was his *duty* to deploy and fight for our country.

He needed to know that I understood that. He ultimately needed to know that I felt a sense of his patriotism and duty was not an either/or choice. He was not choosing the Army, OEF and Afghanistan instead of family. He was going *for* our family. He was going for our nation; for our defense for America's freedoms and for the freedoms and peace of other nations too.

Ryan needed to feel my pride in him for doing his part and serving the U.S. He needed to have a proverbial pat on the back from me knowing that I fully understood the call to arms. He needed my assurance that the fight for justice, and his role as a chaplain to bring spiritual guidance, counsel, and support to his squadron was worthwhile. Ryan was in a unique role to provide opportunities for religious services, practices, and spiritual growth among his unit.

Man! If I had known that was all he needed I think I could have saved us both much turmoil and heartache. Sometimes the simplest of solutions are the hardest to articulate and practice.

Ryan was most able to focus on his mission during the deployment when he knew that I was in full support of it and of him. Did I like him being gone and in a dangerous place? Absolutely not. Could I appreciate and understand his role in this mission? At the time my answer was no. I could not understand.

Looking back, I wish I would have been able to send Ryan off to war with much more of my own confidence in his assignment. My simple blessing was all he needed. My approval and support should have been easy to give. In all of our newfound emotions, I didn't think something so simple would have been the solution.

From My Blog: "Deployment Top 10"

At the end of today, we should be looking at single digits until Ryan returns home. I can't believe it. I have been super frustrated with myself and the number of meltdowns I've had in these last few weeks. Actually, I wouldn't call them meltdowns. I'd call them more like hold-it-all-in-until-the-stress-emits-itself-through-sleeplessness-and-anxiety-attacks. And I don't get it? Why now? Why here at the end?

I have committed to some serious journal writing, some serious attitude adjustments, some serious prayer and Word meditation. And in the spirit of not letting this deployment come to an end without reflection on some of the high points, I am going to do a Top 10 list of the perks of our deployment. I'm trying to see the glass half full, focusing on the benefits of having my husband a world away for the better part of a year.

Number 10: You have supreme and utter dominance over the television and remote in the house, although, I have largely had the television off. I have deleted Ryan's entire DVR line up and I have watched all of the HGTV, New Girl, Glee, Downton Abbey and ABC Family to my heart's content. We only have one television and it has been MINE since the end of December. I am about to relinquish control to college football season, the end of MLB season, NFL season, all manner of shows that deal with finding gold, Alaska, tree logging, antiquing, and border warring. T.V. it was nice knowing you.

Number 9: *Dinner. We have eaten dinner some nights as early as 3:45 or as late as 9:00 pm. We have dined on paper plates and sometimes right out of the nacho box from Casa de Torta. We have had cereal, popcorn, or ramen noodles more nights than I care to admit. We have eaten out at Subway often, driven through Little Caesar's like they were giving away free pizzas, and a few nights we may have even eaten FroYo for dinner. I do enjoy cooking. But when three quarters of the people you are preparing a meal for are just as content with a grilled cheese as they are a four course meal, the choice of what to make is obvious. Ryan doesn't expect giant home cooked meals, but I do it for him anyway when he is here. I am not sure how this will all change. We will probably continue to have some fend-for-yourself nights but I will be glad to make a good meal for at least one person besides myself who will appreciate it. And eat it.*

Number 8: *Tony and Samantha Micilli, who's the boss? I have been the boss. During this deployment, it has been both a negative and a positive experience, but I have made every single decision in this family. From financial decisions, to vehicle decisions, to when and where we eat (see above), to vacations. Yes. What I say goes. Ryan and I are both first born chiefs when it comes to opinions and leadership. I know I have merely done what I've had to do in his absence and am so glad he'll be back to rejoin decision-making. However, I worry that old habits of control will die hard.*

Number 7: *Bob Vila called. He wants his tools back. I have changed out all seven of our smoke alarms. I have removed, cleaned and repaired our dryer's lint screen INSIDE the dryer. I have replaced a*

dead bolt on our front door. I've moved furniture, hauled things to the
dumpster, (attempted to) replace bicycle tires. I've assembled a new
vacuum cleaner and patio furniture. I've dealt with the extermination of
desert insects and van tires that needed replacing. I have come to realize
that you can learn to do just about anything by watching videos on
YouTube. If you are looking for a resume, I can tell you I've neglected it.
But what I do have are a very particular set of skills; skills I have
acquired over a very long deployment.

Number 6: Bravery. I have been married since I was 24 and
although I am by nature a fairly independent person, I have grown
accustomed to the comforts of matrimony. I have meshed easily into the
role of wife; I am comfortable having a husband who leads our home.
But during these last months, I have had to don the Big Girl Panties
(BGP) on several occasions and decide that I can either participate in the
fun of life and be the odd girl out (without her husband), OR I can sit
on the sidelines and watch. I have faithfully taken the kids to church/
chapel, often sitting alone in a pew for the entire service. I have attended
a Couples' Date night at Pine Cove Family Camp this summer as a
singleton. I have driven myself everywhere, opened my own doors and
carried my own bags. I even went to a church Valentine's banquet alone.

Number 5: Friendships. There are some super special gal-pals that
I have absolutely depended on this deployment. There's nothing like
knowing that you can text or call a friend at any hour and know that
she will pray for you, show up at your door with Lysol or Gatorade for
puking kids when you can't leave the house, and she will just get you.

143

These have been the friends that sat with you all basketball season long pretending to watch the games when really you both just needed to bend an ear. These are the friends who will ride with you places and are willing at almost any time to load up the kids and proceed to the next adventure. These are the friends with whom you will trade out play dates, home cooked meals, and babysitting when mama just needs a minute to think. These friends you can just let it all hang out with; the friends who never judge. These are friends who always, always have open arms to hug/give/serve in your hour of need. I know that these deployment friends will always remain close despite the Army's best intentions to scatter us worldwide. But I also know that as our husbands return home, there will be a shift in these friendships. It can't ever be like it was while the guys were deployed. That's just the nature of the beast.

Number 4: Fun. The kids and I have genuinely had some great times in Ryan's absence. We flew home to Tennessee at Christmas. We had fun tubing at the Winter Park and stayed in a great chalet in Ruidoso during the winter. The kids participated in Upward basketball and cheerleading and performed in a music program at church. We all participated in a 5K. Thomas, Mae, and Kate took music lessons on new instruments. We made the best of Christmas, mine and Ryan's birthdays, Valentine's Day, Mother's Day and Father's Day. We held our heads high on the Fourth of July. We had probably the best week of our lives at Pine Cove Family Camp. We enjoyed vacations this summer with both my parents and Ryan's. We traipsed all over the country in the name of killing time this summer and having fun. I certainly hate *that Ryan missed out on that memory making. I'm not sorry that we didn't sit at home and pine away. Life is meant to be lived and living we did!*

Number 3: Me time. This is a strange and surprising item on the list, you may be thinking. In an odd sense, I have had time to focus on my needs that often go unresolved, unmet or get pushed to the back burner in the busyness of life. I have read a whole slew of great books. I have had massages, plural. I have eaten right; enjoyed juicing fruits and vegetables in lieu of cooking a meal. I have made time to get outside and walk just about every day either in the mornings or at dusk; sometimes both. I have gone to bed early or stayed up too late. I have tackled some (fun-to-me) organization projects. I have splurged and saved. I've kept the house clean and I've let it get crazy messy. I've made coffee some mornings and others I've been lazy and reheated it. And still some mornings, I've taken the kids out of the house still in their pajamas for a Starbucks run. I have bought myself flowers at the grocery store many, many weeks. I have rearranged furniture to my liking. I have gone days without shaving my legs. Days! Oh, and Ryan we sleep with a sound machine at night now.

Number 2: Life is not made whole and complete by another person. This goes for kids and husbands and extended family. The only person that fills that God sized void in my life, is in fact God. It has been so easy for me to build idols to the very gifts God has placed in my life: Ryan, Thomas, Mae, and Kate, and even my parents, siblings, and in-laws. But you know what? They can never and will never fulfill me in the way that my one and only first love of Jesus Christ can fill. It's not

145

possible. Oh sure, they bring me joy and happiness and I pray I bring them the same. But I have come to a renewed dependence on the living power of God in ways I have never known in these months of sleepless nights, uncontrollable tears, irrational anxieties, and the aches of loneliness (Deuteronomy. 31:8). It gets easy in the living of our days to think that we hold all of the power and that we determine our course, but how false that notion is! Simply put, I do not know how people survive deployments without the hope and comfort of Christ.

Number 1: By now, you're probably hearing "Chariots of Fire," Kelly Clarkson, Beyonce' or maybe Natasha Bedingfield in the background as an anthem for this post. You'd be right to hear those tunes. Because the number one item on this Top Ten list is that no matter how much you don't believe it; no matter how much you doubt; no matter how much you may have other people who doubt your capability and strength, YOU ARE STRONG. You're not just Hercules strong from all of those sanity-walks, lifting your ladder in and out of the garage, rolling down the full trash and recycle bins each week, mowing the lawn, and carrying sleeping second graders up to bed, but you are inner-strong. You know now that you can do what you thought was impossible. You can do what you didn't dream nine months ago that you'd have the strength to accomplish. You can do anything. Really. And you know that whole "Army Strong" slogan? Well it's meant for you too. Your car breaks down? You get it fixed. You skin a knee? You rub some dirt on it. You fall down? You get back up. You cry yourself to sleep? You awaken the next morning and give today another go. During the deployment, our soldiers earn awards, medals, and honors. We earn our stripes too! The end of our deployment is signaled with a new, deeply-rooted, hard-fought inner confidence that we did it! It isn't over, but it almost is. You hope there won't be another one (deployment) but there might be. You don't want to have to do this again any time soon, but now you know. You can do it. You did do it.

God's Use for the Trial:

For as long as I can remember I have had extreme issues with control. By now and well into your reading, you probably realize that control, the lack of it and what to do with the ensuing emotions is not only a theme of this book, it has been one of the themes of my *entire life*.

Through the difficulties and victories of our deployment, I learned that I have absolutely zero control over God's plans for our lives. He alone knows the future. There is not one ounce of anything I can add to my life by worrying. There is nothing I can gain by keeping a choke-hold on life.

God used the deployment to further highlight how different Ryan and I are and what each of us needed to maintain a healthy relationship as well as personal, mental health during this time. I also believe that the Lord put a reminder in my heart that as John Donne says, "N*o man is an island unto himself.*"

There were so many moments of intense loneliness and worry. There were moments when all I could think of doing was packing up our vehicle to retreat home to our families. The deployment was a true exercise is patience, learning to trust God (again), and looking consciously for the blessings in my life.

I could not have survived this deployment without the strength of my faith in God; without the support and physical help of friends and family members; and without mile markers along the way to count the days, weeks, and months until Ryan came home.

"Houses and wealth are inherited from parents, but a prudent wife is from the Lord...A wife of noble character, who can find? She is worth far more than rubies." {Proverbs 19:14, 31:10}

A mission ready marriage believes it can withstand hard times. It does not simply survive, it thrives.

Questions for Consideration:

1. During a deployment, did your spouses's unit/battalion/ brigade/squad face any casualties? Did this have any effect on either you or your spouse? Are there any long-term affects like depression, sleep disturbances, or Post Traumatic Stress Disorder (PTSD) resulting from this type of tragedy that either of you are possibly still dealing with?

2. What are some of the ways you busy yourself during a deployment? Do you tend to over commit and stay super busy or do you climb under a rock only to emerge once the deployment ends?

3. Have you had any resentment toward your husband for deploying? Unlike me, were you able to give your full blessing for his service and duty or did you ever feel like it was a personal choice between you or the military? How did you overcome this obstacle or misconception?

4. What is the one thing you are most proud of yourself for tackling or handling during a deployment? How did that build confidence and character in you that you still carry with you today?

5. What advice or expertise would you share with a new military spouse before she lives through her first deployment as a dependent? Practically? Spiritually? Financially? Relationally? What helped you the most? What are your pearls of wisdom?

Chapter 8

Reintegration

Those of you with far more military experience than me will find what I am about to say only slightly more ridiculous, ironic, and just plain stupid than how foolish I was about the Army letting us choose where we wanted to be stationed on our first assignment (see Chapter 2).

I failed to listen when people told me that the reintegration process could be difficult, more trying even than the deployment. Maybe for other people, I thought, but not us. Ryan and I love each other. We have a strong marriage. We will just be glad to see each other and resume our lives as normal, I thought. Wide-eyed, I just kept my head high up in the clouds. I did absolutely *no planning* for Ryan's homecoming from Afghanistan other than buying some new lingerie and having a banner professionally printed saying *"Welcome Home!"*

Honestly, I thought life would resume just like it always had been with the exception of me regaling Ryan with all of the fun stories of what he missed and making up for lost time locked away in our bedroom for hours and hours. Except for the bedroom part, I could not have been more wrong.

By far, this chapter of military life is the most painful and difficult for me to write about because it has been the most painful to live through. The months following Ryan's deployment were some of the darkest of my life. And to this day, answers escape me for why it was *so* trying and emotionally agonizing for me. It just was. I can try to pinpoint causes and scapegoats. I can point fingers, but maybe the reintegration was just something I had to go through. Quite possibly, the reintegration period was the means for a necessary spiritual pruning away that I needed.

I had been crying alternating tears of joy and relief since Ryan's plane touched down at the airfield in El Paso. I knew some of that was normal. It was as if all of the emotions and worries I had held in were slowly seeping out with each hug, kiss, conversation, and embrace. I still remember vividly our first argument after Ryan returned home. He got home around midnight on a Thursday and had the weekend to catch up on sleep. Monday morning those on his flight had to report back for loose work/office hours for their ten day reintegration period before any formal leave could be taken. So four days into his time at home and it all started.

The Monday Ryan went into work, he reached for my Nalgene water bottle, filled it up, sealed the lid and proceeded to gather his wallet, keys, and cap on his way out the door. A very real type of lurking, latent anger and "*Oh no he didn't*" bubbled up inside of me.

I asked Ryan why he was taking MY water bottle. He said, "*You're going to be home all day, can't you just drink out of a cup? This will be convenient for me to stay hydrated today.*" And that was the actual conversation. Those were the real words at their face value. But there was something else going on underneath.

What Ryan really meant: "*You're going to be home all day, can't you just drink out of a cup? This will be convenient for me to stay hydrated today.*"

What I really meant: "*You have been gone for nine months. You don't know this, because you haven't been here, but I have been having my daily allowance of water from that water bottle every day. I used it every day you were gone and now you are just going to jack it away from me and pretend like it's your water bottle. You have missed 243 days of me drinking from it and if you'd known that you wouldn't have just whisked my water bottle away to work. You would have left it here. That is just like you. You think the world revolves around YOUR hydration needs, YOUR military career, YOUR deployment, YOUR schedule, what is best for YOU. How dare you take my water bottle? Don't you realize what all I have given up for you in the past nine months? I guess not!!!*"

I can't emphasize enough how affronted I was over that little water bottle incident. It was so silly and simple and stupid. Clearly there were some other issues at play that needed further discussion and attention. Clearly I have moments of being the world's most selfish human alive.

The water bottle incident was just a microcosm of some unresolved issues that would take weeks and months to unfold and unpack. These issues would not disappear magically with the touch down of airplane wheels. Thankfully later that day I went to Target and bought Ryan his own water bottle just like mine and the kids'. And even more importantly, I addressed some of my hidden hurts and frustrations and we were able to continue discussing our expectations and feelings.

I also remember the first several weeks feeling like I didn't want Ryan to leave our sight. I had *simultaneous* feelings of wanting some alone time. It was like I knew I needed some time to myself after having had the sole care of three children for nine straight months, but I felt nearly paralyzed in choosing to be away from Ryan. At the same time, I wanted him to take a turn (or fifty) with parenting our children. But I feared missing out on complete family moments. It was such a time of mixed emotions. Ryan was really darned if he did, darned if he didn't.

I feared that Ryan may have forgotten how we do things around the house, that he wouldn't grasp our new traditions and practices, and that he needed my constant vigilance and smothering oversight. I was growing increasingly overwhelmed and exhausted by all of my self-imposed family gatekeeping.

There were also discussions about our finances; about differing goals for saving and making some large purchases. There were some discussions about expectations; both what I thought Ryan expected of me and what I was expecting of myself as a wife, mother, and woman. And by "discussions" I mean arguments where each of our motives, tones of voice, and intentions were grossly misunderstood.

Keeping this pace was exasperating and exhausting. There were long conversations about Ryan's time in Afghanistan, my worries while he was away, how the casualties and fear had affected us both, and how we had each been able to minister to others during that time. Ryan is one of the world's most easy going persons. He did not come back to us with any real expectations of me, our home or our marrige. His primary emotions were those of gratitude and relief for all of the ways I had held our life together in his absence.

My primary reactions were mental fragility, emotional sensitivity, and being on the precipice of falling apart. And it became a vicious cycle. I could not for the life of me figure out why I just couldn't be happy and thankful that Ryan was home. He was healthy, uninjured, and mentally and spiritually strong. He returned to me unscathed in every way. But I continued to slip further and further down a disparaging hole of the reintegration. Debilitating anxiety was wrapping its fingers around me.

I continued to battle the *"What ifs"* of Ryan's safety and of mine and the kids making it through the deployment. Instead of saying, *"Thank you Lord, it's over!"* I would reason that yes, we had survived but fixate on wondering about what if we hadn't. That was a highly unfruitful place to let my mind linger and dwell.

I began to withdraw from the very friendships that were my lifelines from late December of 2012 until August of 2013. I had heard that your friendships would never be the same once the soldiers returned home and it was coming true. It was as though we were all glad to have each of our families under one roof again so the impromptu dinner plans, park play dates, and battle buddy time simply vanished.

In a way, I know that is how it is supposed to be, but in another way I know I was mourning that loss. How could those ladies who had become my life-lines suddenly no longer be a vital part of my days? How could the graces of God through feminine fellowship so abruptly vanish into thin air?

I wish that I had made more of an effort to maintain those friendships instead of cutting them off so dramatically. I even mistakenly pulled away from other outlets that had been crucial to my overall sanity and mental health. I quit going to my PWOC Bible study and I basically sat around the house each day (save for a handful of the kids' activities) and waited on Ryan to get home from work. I was in an unhealthy rhythm of being available to Ryan and being hyper-vigilant to his perceived needs. I had missed him for nine months. It had become my number one goal to be available around the clock so that we could resume our lives together.

It was also during this time, our unit experienced two self-inflicted casualties in the very same weekend. I will spare the difficult and disturbing details. As the unit chaplain, our family, and Ryan in particular, was very much involved in the details of these tragedies. The fallout, grief counseling of other soldiers, command meetings, plans for funeral arrangements, memorial services, prevention strategies for further incidents of similar proportions all fell to Ryan. These were not just casual acquaintances of his. These were his friends, his comrades, his brother and sister in arms. These were fellow service members, precious to Ryan.

It was demands and stresses of the job like these that continued to push me away from Ryan. I kept my own anxiety over these tragic circumstances to myself. I isolated my feelings and barely clung to my faith in a God that suddenly felt distant and far off. I figured that me sharing my internal battles with Ryan would only burden him more. On the outside I may have looked like I was keeping things together; on the inside I was an emotional wreck and barely functioning. My mind was hardly shutting down at night, sleep was becoming scarce, and twinges of paranoia would send me into a panic. I continued to isolate myself against my friends and family.

This personal time of transition and re-establishing our new rhythms was a largely painful time for me. I may never know what ultimately caused these feelings of desperation and many sleepless nights. I can guess and speculate that it was a combination of things. It was exhaustion, unrealistic expectations, a release of some very real and extremely heavy emotions and adrenaline. That was paired with mourning the loss of life, mourning the change and frequency of friendships, and a mix of joy and relief at Ryan's return. I was also grieving some of my languishing independence and confidence from surviving the deployment.

What I Needed:

I probably should have gone to see a counselor, pastor or therapist. It is a Catch-22 when your husband is a chaplain. He is a counselor and pastor but he is not MY counselor or pastor. He is my husband. There is no way for him to objectively help me process my emotions when so many of them surround him and our own marriage.

It would have benefitted me immensely to have a weekly appointment with someone knowledgeable in these matters. It would have even been wise to sit down with a seasoned military wife or friend to intentionally process these emotions, feelings, and difficulties. As a chaplain's spouse, and someone who whole-heartedly believes that I am ministering and serving our military community alongside and *with* Ryan, I believed that *I* was supposed to be the one helping others. I held a foolish belief that asking for help for myself was a sign of indulgence and weakness.

During a time when there was a definite need for some care for the care-giver, I chose to suffer silently and attempt to handle my problems on my own. I falsely believed the lie that my emotional heartaches didn't matter to anyone. I even wondered if they mattered to God.

Too often I have made an untrue assumption that I have been put on this Earth to help manage, serve, and meet the needs of others. When it is my turn to fall apart, (as we are all entitled every now and again), I think I am bothering or inconveniencing others to share my own needs. I have often heard the phrase that *"Isolation is desperation."* And I believe it is absolutely true. The biggest mistakes I made after Ryan's homecoming included thinking:

- that everything would be fine and normal, surely nothing had changed between us.
- I could handle these confusing and peculiar feelings all on my own.
- I no longer needed those friends and relationships I spent nine months building, Ryan was home now.
- I could just pretend like I was fine, surely this dark cloud would eventually pass.
- I must be the only woman and spouse who has ever felt like this, surely something was wrong with me and I was not normal.
- (*again*) that maybe I was just not cut out for this role as a military spouse.

What He Needed:

One of the worst assumptions I made and could have ever presumed was that Ryan getting home would be the answer to every single problem, worry, or emotion in my life. That was one of the most unfair things I have inadvertently and subconsciously asked of Ryan in our entire marriage. Unfortunately, I had become somewhat lax in the practices of prayer and Bible reading while Ryan was away. I had made Ryan's homecoming my god and the answer to all of my feelings and concerns.

Ryan needed me to allow him to simply be my husband and partner. It was unfair of me to extend such unreasonable expectations and assumptions for who and what he needed to be in my life. It was also unreasonable for me to set such crazy expectations of myself in assuming I could be Ryan's everything too.

It was that ugly perfectionism and striving that reared its' nasty head in my direction. I believe that if I could just transform myself into the perfect wife and fill every need and void for Ryan that our life and marriage would be perfect. He never expected me to wait around the house on him. By no means did he expect me to dream up and whip up Barefoot Contessa dinners each night after he had survived nine months on Army food. Ryan never insisted for me to keep our house spotless and perfect. He did not need me to grill him every afternoon when he walked in the door from work. I had *chosen* to give up many of my own hobbies and activities the day Ryan stepped off the plane. That was on me. It was very unfair to Ryan for me to hover over him, smother him, and insist on such vigilance toward his every move as a husband and father.

Perfectionistic and compulsive behaviors can make life miserable for everyone. I was definitely miserable. At what should have been a sweet time in our marriage to wrestle with gentleness and kindness toward one another, I turned into a time of extreme tension and mutual frustration.

I had started walking straight for the deep end of crazy. Most crucially, I now know that Ryan needed me to take the proper means necessary to regain my own mental health in order to be "myself" again. This weird, isolated, depressed person was of no help to our marriage or my mothering. Ryan offered on multiple occasions to help get me in touch with someone I could talk to or meet with (counselor) but I kept refusing. Instead I kept staying up all hours of the night, restless and anxious. I kept writing frantically in my journal, holding my breath and moving toward a very dark emotional place. I kept pushing down high anxiety by pacing the house at night, taking multiple walks during the day, and trying to allow months of pent-up fear, worry, and adrenaline escape my body.

Ryan also suggested that maybe I see my primary care physician and have a physical to discuss the possible need for some medicinal intervention. Again, I refused. I was living with near constant restlessness and mental distress along with bouts of languishing depression. I projected my own misery onto everyone in my house. It was not fun to be around me during this time.

From My Blog: "My Word: Finish"

I have been faithful all year to select a word for each month. These words have been words to live by. These words have anchored me; they have inspired me; they have kept this year moving. I have basically shut down my blog to anyone reading besides me. I have also sparsely posted. I have just not had the heart, energy, or "umph" to do so.

But I have missed the benefits of therapeutic writing. And I have been disappointed with myself that I have gone strong for 11 months and here at month 12, I've almost walked away. So despite the fact that I haven't written much, I have certainly been thinking much, feeling much, and processing much.

This year, 2013, has been a year of toil. It has been a year of living in "fight or flight" mode for the many months Ryan was gone. Despite believing that all of life's problems would be solved the moment he stepped off a plane, life and its problems have just continued coming and at times have felt heavier than the time Ryan was away. The waiting I did on Ryan's return has now turned into the waiting for my stresses and worries and adrenaline to just seep away. I say all of this to say, in the deepest recesses of my heart, I know that this too, shall pass.

These feelings of exhaustion, depression, anxiety, and of waiting for the storms to pass will eventually move on. The fog will clear. I know it. I am thankful that we have had a chance to spend a few weeks with family. I am thankful that we are getting a chance to rest, relax, sleep in, and just chill. No agendas. No real plans.

I pray that as we make our way back to El Paso that we will return refreshed. And I pray that I will be able to joyfully, and thankfully, welcome a new year, 2014. I believe that just turning the page on 2013's calendar will make a world of difference. It will be a time of new beginnings. A year of new (but welcome) changes. A year of moving. A year of closure, but also a year of meeting new people; restarting our life in a new place.

So My Word for December is simply this, finish. I want to finish this year out strong. I want to finish this year with my head up and position myself to have my heart looking up too. God is so faithful to me, to us, to our family. "And I am sure of this, that He who began a good work in you will bring it to completion at the day of Jesus Christ." (Philippians 1:6)

God's Use for the Trial:

I cannot reiterate enough just how uncomfortable, isolating, and lonely this time in my life was. If I had to choose a few words to describe it I would use confused, doubtful, joyless, and anxious. Confused would have to top the list. It just didn't make sense to me that at a time when joy and relief should have been my primary emotions, I could not seem to find either.

I wanted Ryan's help around the house, but I wanted him to do it my way. I wanted Ryan to rejoin in the parenting, but I wanted to tell him how I'd been doing it. I wanted Ryan to take over our finances and big decision making, but I was personally offended when he didn't handle things the way I had been handling them. I wanted Ryan to communicate with me, but I also wanted him to leave me alone. I wanted Ryan around but I needed my space. I loved having him back in our bed, but his snoring kept me awake all hours of the night. I wanted date nights and romance, but at times I felt distant and lacked those old feelings of intimacy. I couldn't quite articulate what was going on and I know Ryan, of all people, was equally confused. I needed God to show up and quickly!

Here is the truth: I serve a FAITHFUL God and He did show up. I will admit, it did not feel dramatic or grand at the time. I failed see Him write in the clouds or send me a personal message. I certainly didn't hear an audible voice, or thundering clouds or see lightning strike.

What I did experience was God's steady faithfulness every day when I woke up. What I did feel in my direst moments was a God who continued to whisper *"Don't give up,"* and *"I love you and have a plan for your life,"* and *"You are My beloved and My chosen daughter."* In my desperation I felt His tugs on my heart that He would never leave or forsake me. I felt His assurance in the sunrise each day that He would continue to give me the grace I needed for that day, that hour, that moment. I felt God's faithfulness when a few trusted friends would tell me, *"You will get beyond this."* And I felt it often when apologies were made and forgiveness was extended by a sweet, tender husband.

God would continue to prove Himself over and over and over as I did finally began to slowly and incrementally feel the emotional clouds leave and the sun shine again. I began to realize that Christ alone is the Lover of my soul and the Restorer of my joy.

It was in Him and through Him that Ryan safely made it back from Afghanistan. It was in Him and though Him that Thomas, Mae, Kate and I survived as well. It is in Christ Jesus that I have freedom from sin and death, and victory in this life. I just thought all of the tough lessons I would learn about myself and my faith would be contained *within* the timeframe of the deployment itself. This was not the case at all. I learned more of God's faithfulness and sovereignty in the months that followed. Even when I had to strain to see or feel Him, I knew it was the hands of a loving God that were carrying me through.

"The steadfast love of the Lord never ceases; His mercies never come to an end; they are new every morning; great is Your faithfulness." {*Lamentations 3:22-23*}

A mission ready marriage acknowledges the need for help and takes the proper means for getting it.

Questions for Reflection:

1. Have you ever faced difficulties in your marriage following a deployment? How did this surprise you? How did you handle the challenges?

2. Has there ever been a time that you, as a military spouse have had a "mission related" or "combat stress related" near-breakdown? How did you come back from it? What helped you to cope during this season of adversity?

3. At the heart of my challenges with Ryan's reintegration was (again) my need for believing I was in control, my unrealistic expectations of myself and Ryan, and the ultimate refinement of my faith. What spiritual fruit did you bear as a result of similar demands? How long did the process take for you?

4. I am a firm believer that God lets none of our experiences go to waste. As difficult as it sometimes is to undergo such a process of refining and growth, would you ever forego those seasons and give them up even if it meant a stagnancy in your faith? Why or why not?

5. Think about a very specific time you have had to cling to God's promises. Explain exactly how you saw His handprints of faithfulness in your life. Maybe He is still working out the details in a situation you are presently going through. Envision the praises you will give Him when He faithfully, eventually brings you out of your darkness.

Chapter 9

Moving? So Soon?

Looking back I can see with the wisdom of hindsight that much of my mental and emotional discombobulation upon Ryan's return from Afghanistan had multiple culprits. One of the major clouds hanging over my head was the fact than in less than six months after Ryan's return, we were met with Request For Orders (RFO) for a move, or Permanent Change of Station (PCS).

This news was not sprung upon us. Before he got started at Fort Bliss we were aware that for Ryan's rank as a chaplain, most duty assignments lasted between two and a half to three years. We acknowledged that our time was coming in the late spring/summer of 2014 to make a move.

On one hand, we were ecstatic. We were thrilled to close one chapter of our military career and move into the next. We were thrilled to have closure with one unit experience and welcome a new one. We were excited to meet new friends, explore a new area, and (*fingers crossed*) move back closer to our families. There would be a new house, a new neighborhood, and more fresh starts for our entire family.

What many non-military people fail to understand about life on the cusp of a military move, is that one can be simultaneously filled with great joy and sadness over a PCS. There is joy and excitement over crossing the finish line for one assignment. There is joy as you are filled with apprehension over the possibilities and novelty of your next duty station.

At the exact *same time*, you feel sadness and grief over the goodbyes and what will be lost among friends and the place where you have made your home. There is sadness knowing that sometimes the first months at a new place can be lonely and filled with a steep learning curve. I can see why I felt crazy much of the time. In that interim of knowing you have orders coming but realizing that it could literally be ANYWHERE in the world that the Army is sending you, it can be hard to focus on little else. For those of us who already struggle in the land of *"What-ifs"* the not knowing is pure torture.

Once you know your location and you have official orders it is really difficult not to let the logistical demands take over your mind. There is much to consider. You are dually closing out one life and opening up another. There is your current home to clean, purge, sell/rent/or clear post from. There is the new housing arrangement to set up. And in our case, we were SO far geographically from one duty station to the next, it was not practical to physically visit our new place too far ahead of our report date.

Then there are important decisions to be made about schooling options, work, childcare, what to get involved in. There are church decisions, budgeting issues to revisit, and overall concerns about how everyone is going to fare in the new city. There are utilities to shut off and turn on elsewhere, accounts to manage, and a myriad of planning details that the grownups have to consider.

As a woman who thrives on organization, efficiency, and serves as the manager of the home, a relocation can top the list of stressful life situations. There is so much at stake in the important decisions. It's easy to feel that much of our identity, potential happiness, and future quality of life is wrapped up in making informed choices.

It is not just about *where* we live. Decisions about our homes (neighborhoods, price, nearby amenities, school zoning, distance to work and the grocery store and much more) are all weighty decisions. These nuances factor heavily into what kind of life we will have in our new town. Unfortunately, for most military families, we rarely get much notice about moving and once we do know some details we often have even less time to make these final, monumental arrangements.

We all desire the best quality of life we can afford and can financially handle. I think this truth is even more exacting among military families. You have to find your new rhythm fast and then just get into the groove as soon as possible. When you know you will only live somewhere two or three years (or often less) you want to dig in and start planting some roots.

In competitive real estate markets we may have to act quickly to secure a place. Military families hardly have the luxury of languishing over decisions about relocation. You just get to a place mentally where you make a choice, go with it and start to get on with life at your next assignment. You sign a lease, take the post housing offered, or put in an offer on a home for sale; sometimes sight unseen. You get the keys and start unloading your life off the truck and into the new space.

It can be excruciatingly unnerving and easy to second guess yourself. You immediately wonder if you have chosen the right zip code, the right schools, the right neighborhood. Is it too far for your husband to commute to and from work every day? Is it too much a part of the military community or too little? Is this a good thing or bad? Do my new neighbors seem friendly or normal? Will I be close to the grocery store or a 24-hour pharmacy? What about restaurants and cultural opportunities like plays and museums and concert venues?

And the *most* crucial question of all, *"Where is the nearest Target?"*

With so much of your time being filled trying to make these connections from afar or via the Internet in the months leading up to your move, it is certainly easy to become distracted in the life right in front of you where you are. The emotions run high and it becomes increasingly difficult to figure out what parts of your heart are here and what parts are there. I think I have finally realized that it is normal for your heart to be divided and for pieces and parts of us to be scattered all about.

What I Needed:

I believe that it was natural for me to begin emotionally pulling away from El Paso and my friendships when I did. After all, over half of my closest military friends had already begun to move away before we did. In this crazy military cycle you always find yourself in a different place. Some months you are the new kid, others you are right smack-dab in the middle, and before too much longer, you are the short-timer.

If I had to do it all again I would have tried much harder to maintain all of my connections (PWOC Bible study, homeschool moms, unit friends, and chapel friends) right up until the day we pulled out of town. I acted out of inexperience in handling our situation like I did. I thought it would surely be easier to just slowly and gradually fade away from El Paso and that maybe if I quit participating in many of my obligations and engagements, no one would notice; no one would care; no one would miss me and saying goodbye would be easier.

There is no easy goodbye. And as divided as your heart can be over the anticipation of your next adventure and mourning the losses of your current one, the best thing I could have done was to BE PRESENT. I needed to have stayed in the todays instead of worrying about too many tomorrows and what may lay ahead in Georgia.

When so much feels out of our control, some of us resort to our fleshly nature of trying to be *in* control. In getting so focused on what was next: the next job for Ryan, the next city, the next house, the next school opportunities for our kids I lost sight of the gift of the present. I had the idea that if I could just search out the Internet, make enough lists and check them all twice (or ten times) that I was keeping a handle on my circumstances and feelings in the final lines of an important life chapter. It's wise to make plans but I needed to keep focus on the blessings that were still to behold at my current place.

When I got in a mental upheaval with all of my conflicting emotions about saying goodbye to dear friends, our old house and three years worth of memories, my need to control the details of our relocation got ugly. I needed to remember that I wasn't in control. Ryan wasn't in control. The Army (really) wasn't in control. It was God who was in control of the great and small details. As is always the case, He just needs me to trust Him.

What He Needed:

In our relationship Ryan is clearly the laid back, easy going of the two. I bet you couldn't have guessed *that* by now. I tend to be the worrier and the manager of tiny details. Moving to a new place can easily send me into a tailspin before we've even begun the real work of relocating.

As I was beginning to work myself into an emotional tizzy, Ryan sensed my frazzled state. He is the head of our home, and he is the actual employee of the United States government. He has the emails, the orders and inside scoop. I think at some point he needed me to get off of his proverbial back and let him take the reins. It's most definitely a two person job to square away a relocation, but in this case he (and I both) needed us to have a plan so he could stay in his lane and I could stay in mine.

After preliminary research (online) and talking to some trusted friends, we narrowed down our housing situation for Georgia. I'm not here to discuss the advantages and disadvantages of each, but for this duty station we agreed that we wanted to rent a home off post. Once that decision was made, we carefully looked at the numbers in our budget and came to an agreement on what we could comfortably afford. We were able to find an area of town that met our budget parameters and also our needs for convenience to post and family activities.

As our travel situation was somewhat complicated, Ryan just finally stepped in and made the final decision. It turned out that about two weeks ahead, I would be able to make a quick trip to our new town alone and secure housing. We had a short list of rentals in a very specific neighborhood. I was setting up appointments with realtors and property managers to make the most of a short visit. Ryan would stay back in El Paso while the house was packed out and meet me and the kids at our new place.

By doing things this way (a way I didn't see as initially practical), we were able to get into our new house the day we all drove into town. We received our household goods (HHG) only two days later. There were no hotels and no extra expenses of eating out for weeks on end. It was a very smooth move.

Ryan held a few more pieces of the puzzle this time and by allowing him the room to function as the head of our home and the principal big decision maker, I was able to relax a little. The end result was a peaceful, easy transition out of El Paso and into our new life awaiting us outside of Augusta, GA.

From My Blog: "Good Enough is Great"

I have a million little to-do, to-get, to-buy, to-pack, to-bring lists going. One of the things I have planned out for these last remaining weeks in El Paso is to deep clean everything in the house. I want to leave our home in good shape for whomever may inhabit it next. We have planned to hire professional cleaners once our belongings are out, but I won't be there for that so I want to do what I can now.

Friday we came straight home from the kids' last PE class and I planned to start on windows, window treatments, and blinds in my bedroom. Next week, I'll work on the kids' windows and downstairs. First, I stripped my bed, and washed our sheets. I removed all of my curtains, removed the hardware and rods, bagged and secured all pieces together; I removed the blinds, gave them a bath in warm water and ammonia, cleaned my windows and window seals. Finally I put the blinds back up and reminded myself how much I won't miss all of the dust and dirt that gets blown in here in El Paso.

To me, naked windows are a sure sign of transition. That seems to be one of the final things I do once we settle in to a new place and one of the first things to start taking down when we leave. It makes me happy but sad at the same time. We have four windows and a single French door that leads to a small balcony in our bedroom. It took a while to get it all done yesterday, but now that it's all down, the room feels so open and bare and bright.

Thankfully, I'd planned to let our dinner Friday come from the Crock-pot because I got in a deep clean of our oven too. If I have any dirty, dark secrets it's got to be my oven. Seriously, I never clean it. And it gets used almost daily. And it was gross; so, so embarrassingly gross. So it was time to get out the Brillo pads and elbow grease.

I even needed a head light to really get in there to see. In my next life, I want to come back rich so I can hire a housekeeper; one who will regularly clean our large appliances.

I was literally up to my hands and elbows in oven gunk when I saw where I'd missed a call from a realtor who wants to show our house Saturday around noon. Yay!!! That good news added extra motivation so I kept on scrubbing and wiping and getting all of the stainless steel shining and bright. I went to bed bone-tired from a day of work but also happy and hopeful that we have another home showing. I had a big chunk of housework finished, but know that today (Saturday) there's plenty more to get the house "show ready."

Our house has been on the market close to 50 days. And today will be only our second showing. We know that there's a big influx of military people that will be arriving this summer so we are trying not to fret. We are trying to be patient with this process. However, I have grown fairly weary in keeping our house so neat and orderly. I like it picked up and clean anyway, but keeping it ready to show at all times can be exhausting. I hate feeling like I'm always reminding the kids to make sure their rooms are impeccably spotless. We literally don't leave home with an unmade bed or the toilet lid up. We have all of our towels folded, pillows fluffed, sink empty and our counters wiped to perfection. And I'm tired!

Then I start second guessing our actual house. I try and see it as a buyer would see it. What about it is a turn-off? What about it seems unlivable to someone else? Our neighborhood is modest. It's nothing fancy but full of houses and people that make living in Redstone wonderful. Our neighbors have been outstanding. It's a quiet area with lots of military families, retirees, and para-military professionals (law enforcement and border patrol). People park in their garages and driveways. The streets are not crowded with millions of cars. Although it's a new neighborhood, all of the construction is finally complete; so no more loud noise, Mariachi music, and construction vehicles coming in and out. We have an HOA that has helped to maintain neat yards, sidewalks, and the overall appearance of the neighborhood.

When we bought our house, I had all of these visions of mornings spent on our balcony having coffee. But we have never used that balcony. Not once. But we have used the little nook on the front of the house. There have been many cups of coffee consumed, many porch dates, many chapters of the Bible read, many phone calls to loved ones there, and many, many hours of conversations and watching our kids play out front. The blessing of military life is that you get the opportunity to live in many, many houses. You find out quickly what you love and what you don't love about each particular house. Such is true for us with our El Paso home.

Some of the very things that drive me crazy about this house are also the things that I love about it. For example, you walk in our front door and you're in the whole downstairs. We have no foyer, no entry, no hallway. Boom, you're inside. I didn't even pay that much attention to this detail until once we moved in. On the one hand I hate it. I hate that I can't hide our mess. I hate that you walk in and you see the sink, the kitchen, the den. But at the same time I love that about this house. We have a wall of windows that has made my comfort level with the kids playing outside unsupervised, very high.

While we do hope to have a house with a second living area in our next house, I have loved that we came here as a family of five. We were all we had. We had each other. This house has forced us to watch the same television shows, snuggle on the same couches, and fellowship together. When we are schooling, some can work at the table, some at the island, some spread out on the rug. And I am in the same room. I can multitask like nobody's business with this floor plan. As someone who cooks often and enjoys it, I have loved being virtually in the same room as my family during meal preparation and clean up.

This floor plan has kept me accountable. This floor plan has forced me to keep a tidy house. This in turn has made me more open to hospitality. When your house stays tidy, you're much more likely to invite your neighbor inside for coffee, you are more likely to welcome in the neighborhood kids for pizza or popsicles, and host dinner for friends. Our downstairs is literally one, giant multipurpose room. We eat, study, rest, veg-out, read, discuss, plan, laugh, cry, love...all in one open space.

Maybe I was channeling my inner Caroline Ingalls when we found this house. Maybe I figured if a one-room living area was good enough for Ma then it must be good enough for me. When there's only one place to gather as a family, it does a family good!

I have loved and hated our kitchen island as well. I have loved the giant counter space for meal prep, to school plan, to feed the kids, to have as a serving bar. But lately I have reverted to letting the kids eat most of their meals here. It's just been too easy especially when Ryan and I have been having dinner later than the kids. We haven't needed a formal dining room. And I have also loved that just as I can see right out the front of the house, I can also see right into our back yard. Having the big rock wall has been nice for privacy as well as a nice area that I can turn the kids loose and know that they are safe. On this small back porch we have had Wood Academy of Christian Kids (WACK) celebrations, we've done science experiments, and we've brought our school work and lunches outside.

Although it has often been brown more than it has been green, I'm glad Ryan decided to sod the back yard anyway. In a city where there isn't much green, it's been nice to have a small patch on our property. Yes, this house has been a great home for us. It's easy to start running through the list of "not-good-enoughs" when it's time to let other people in to see where you live. It's easy to feel like your house is less than with counters or blinds that you don't feel measure up. Or that someone may not like walking right in and seeing the kitchen sink, or worrying that the open floor plan is too much or not enough of this or that.

It's easy to second guess all of the things you have loved about your house when someone else is making judgments on it. But today, as I do the final finishing touches on getting the house "show ready" I will continue to pray that the right family comes through here. I will continue to pray that we have a buyer because I know God brought us here and He will make a way when it's time for us to leave. I will continue to pray that others will see this house as so much more than stucco and windows and tile floors and kitchen islands. I pray that those families who come through our house will see a home. I pray that they will see this place as their home; a place where their own memories can be made. A place where love and peace and comfort and retreat can abide. A place where the highs and lows, the joys and sorrows can be shared. A place for the tired and weary to find rest. A place for the hungry to find fullness. A place where life just doesn't happen, but a place where a life is lived; and an abundant life is made.

I prayed all of those things for us when we started our journey here in El Paso. And those things have certainly been true of our dwelling here at Redstone Pass Court. And I continue to pray those things over our next house that awaits us in Georgia. Has this been our dream house? No. Are there a dozen things we'd do differently if we had to do it over again? Absolutely. Have we lived and learned here? You bet. Home really is where the heart is. And our good enough house has really been a great home.

God's Use for the Trial:

If nothing else, I think moving and relocating does a few things for our spiritual growth. This can ultimately also help our marriages grow stronger as well. I believe that all of the chaos and details and worry keeps us in a steady relationship with serious dependency on God.

While we wait for orders, we know that ultimately God is the one who calls us to our next assignment. He has good and mighty plans for us there and despite the fact that the Army sends the snail mail with the orders and location announced, I firmly believe God chooses where He wants us. I believe this for the jobs and duties He will have our husbands perform within their units. I believe this for the areas of influence He gives us as spouses, and I also believe it holds true for our children.

While we live in the disarray and turmoil of a cluttered house in transition, we are dependent upon God for our peace of mind and our mental focus. While we transition from one community of friendships to another, we keep our eyes fixed on Jesus because we know above all He goes before us and He has our neighborhoods, friendships, and circles of our people already ordained and ordered.

Moving and relocating reminds us of the temporal nature of all things. Our homes are temporary, some of our relationships are seasonal, and most of all our troubles in this life are momentary. We often hear the familiar lament that *"God never gives us more than we can handle."* In light of the trials and bedlam associated with moving from one city to the next, it is God who helps us handle what He gives.

Finally, I believe that the Lord uses these seasons of moving on and starting over (again) as graces to each of us to make fresh starts and new beginnings. We have chances unlike many of our civilian counterparts to continue reinventing ourselves. We are given small gifts each time we take on another new "permanent" change of station to reaffirm our strengths, to refresh our homes and our style, to reawaken passions either personal, artistic, professional, and in our marriages too.

Most of all, we are given a new chance to regenerate our relationship with Christ. We can continue to walk by faith and not by sight. We can continue to trust in His unfailing provision even among all of the tiny, minuscule, and mundane details.

"Therefore if anyone is in Christ, he is a new creation. The old has passed away; behold the new has come." {2 Corinthians 5:17}

A mission ready marriage enjoys the blessings of the past, stays grounded in the present, & delights in the future.

Questions for Reflection:

1. In your opinion, what is the most difficult part about waiting for orders? What tops your list as some of the first things you accomplish or put on your to-do list once you know you are moving?

2. What do you think the advantages are of each choice we have in terms of housing? Do you prefer living on post? Off post? Renting? Buying? Have you had any horror stories or huge wins with one preference over another?

3. What specifically do you do to prevent that natural pulling away from friendships until the final days of leaving your current city? How do you cope with saying goodbye? Do you have any fun traditions or ways you celebrate the closing of a chapter at an old place or the beginning of a new chapter at your upcoming duty station?

4. In your marriage, what tends to be the division of labor and/or worry about all of the necessary details that a PCS entails? Which of you is the worrier? The calm, cool cucumber? The doer, the thinker, the realist?

5. What would you say are the biggest advantages and challenges of moving every few years? What specifically do you see God doing in your life and marriage as a result of having this opportunity/burden? How do you hope to grow or use this as a means for spiritual development?

Chapter 10
The Art of Reinventing Yourself...Again

While there is much excitement in fresh starts and new beginnings in a different place, this transition can also be met with the daunting and ongoing task of reinventing yourself, again. This takes on the form of finding a new community, again. It means keeping professional ties and certifications and connections current, again. It can mean searching for that illusive job that may or may not ever materialize. It can mean finding new routes around town, your nearest grocery store, a new dentist, primary care provider and hair stylist. Did I mention finding a new hair stylist? The hardest lesson I learn again each time we move is figuring out how I will reinvent myself as a friend in a new community.

We are still fairly new in our military service but I can't help but empathize with those spouses who after so many moves, just finally throw in the towel and decide they don't have it in them one more time to put themselves out there. I hope and pray I don't ever resort to that, but I get it. I do. It's tiresome to the soul.

Each of us has different God given traits, personalities, and temperaments. I happen to be what I like to call an extroverted introvert. I love to get out there and meet people, and make many new friends. But I also know the value and my need for a handful of real, true friends who I can count on. I need a close inner circle with whom I can share my heart, struggles, and victories.

I firmly believe that our spouses should be our truest confidants. We should nurture that relationship foremost. However, as military spouses the reality is that our husbands just aren't always around or available. I have found that having a few close confidants and Christian sisters is absolutely necessary to my own mental and emotional health.

Like most things of any value, friendships take time to establish. Consider the metaphor of a garden. We must plant seeds and then water and nurture them, expose them to sunlight, and wait. Our harvest takes time. There is much tending to be done. As much as most of us like to jump right in and make our new place our home for the next few years, there is an art to friendship and it can't be fabricated in a day or a week or even a month. This process not only happens slowly, it can be painstaking too.

After our most recent PCS I found myself ready to do the necessary work to make new friends. I know that making a friend requires being a friend and I began showing up at the places where I knew the types of friends I need could be found.

I went to the summer PWOC Bible study. I went to the park play date/ meet-and-greet for our area homeschoolers. I went to the first of our unit coffees as well as the chaplain spouses' coffee and Unit Ministry Team (UMT) summer cookout. I smiled, shook hands, and carefully remembered names, details, anecdotes and so began a few connections. We also began attending an off post church where we knew a few family acquaintances. We joined a small group from that church and met all of our neighbors. For those of us with children, this process is amplified in that we are doing this not only for ourselves, but also for them.

I connected with a few people on Facebook and social media and even exchanged phone numbers with a few new acquaintances. This for me, is the easy part. I have no problems or issues with meeting, greeting, and small talk. I can do that with ease. I know that isn't the case for many women. Those parts that come easily to me can be excruciating to others. Insecurities, social anxieties, and down right intimidation can cause many of us to feel that the trouble of making new relationships just isn't worth it.

In the first few months in a new place I always say my friendships are a mile wide and an inch deep. I wish I could be satisfied with just having a pool of friendly acquaintances.

I wish I could be happy just knowing I may run into someone I've met at the library or grocery store. I wish it would suffice for me to simply be content with small-talking with other moms and women at homeschool and chaplain events. But that's not me. I need deep connections with at least a few people. I need to be able to be honest, open, and transparent. I just can't fake it all of the time and need a small constituency of close companions with whom to walk through each season of my life.

The beauty of our military life is that we can have a few of these close friends everywhere we go. Just because I've moved doesn't mean that Kelly, Amy, Ginger, Tiffany, or Cathy aren't dear friends any longer. The reality is that once you aren't in the same geographical place, the dynamics of the friendships change and are altered.

The first few months of being the new girl again can be exhausting. It often feels like with every introduction you are condensing your life story down into just a few short sentences or bullet points on a resume. And within those few moments you are trying to convey a sense of your worth as a woman, a professional, a mother, a wife or quite frankly as just a normal human being. Assuming the initial introduction goes well and you have a chance to continue building into a budding friendship, the next phase can be equally as tiring. At least for me, I try to be hospitable. I open my home for a play date or coffee. This is an opportunity to get to know a new friend better; kind of a second date if you will. But so often, after some longer conversations and face to face interaction, you may realize that your ideals aren't exactly aligned or your interests or personalities just don't jibe.

When you realize that maybe this friendship isn't a match and that it won't move beyond a casual association, you know that you're going to have to keep looking and essentially begin the whole process again. Sometimes you're the one that pulls away gently and at other times the other friend is just not that into *you*. Either way, this process can be painful and leave you emotionally spent.

Maybe this sounds superficial or needy on my part, but it's just another layer of transitioning to a new place. Certainly, not everyone you meet will be a lifelong best friend. But I, at least, have to go through this process because otherwise nearly everyone you meet will forever linger in the acquaintance zone. This process can be similar for job interviews, finding new practitioners, and generally settling into life some place new.

After several weeks and months of this you just start to wear down. You start to question if it really is worth it to invest the time, energy, and heart into finding a cohort of those with whom you share a close rapport and affinity. I honestly question my value as a friend. I wonder if people see me as I am. Do they think I have something to offer or think I am worth getting to know. After all, I'll only live someplace a few years and people who know I'm not permanently apart of their community may not feel like I am worth the investment of their time. I quickly get very insecure during these first few months of the reinvention phase. I get frustrated and I get tired.

I get tired of trying to prove myself. I get tired of the lonely feelings because I've known the sweetness and joys of deep friendships. I don't go long down that trail of thought before I remember that I don't function well in isolation. I therefore continue to go the extra mile in building inroads with a few women with whom my values, interests and ideals match.

How many times have you tried one hair stylist only to realize you have to keep looking? Or you have found a new dentist only to realize he or she isn't the right one for your family. Maybe you have accepted a job or a position of leadership in a volunteer role only later to discover that it wasn't the right fit. Over and over we must continue evaluating ourselves and our circumstances. Over and over we must remain patient to find our niches, positions, and places of comfort.

What I Needed:

During this phase I always need several reminders. I need to be reminded that my worth isn't found in the friends I make. I need to be reminded that in Christ I have all I need. I am enough; my marriage is enough; my children are enough. Honestly, there are days you feel like you are in junior high school again. Navigating the social waters can be tricky. I need frequent reminders that I am individually me and I don't need to change that to fit or conform into someone else's idea of what a friend looks like.

I need the reminder that I am not reduced to a bulleted resume list of my best qualities. I am fearfully and wonderfully made by a Creator who thinks I am unique and special. God thinks that even when others may not see it in me or I may not see it in myself.

I also need to be reminded that patience is not only a virtue but also it is a Fruit of the Spirit (Galatians 5:22-23). Cultivating patience in the area of making new friends, finding a new job, or social activities are some of the ways the Lord keeps our hearts attuned to His. Just like the houses, neighborhoods, and duty stations He ordains for us, I know that He goes before us, too, in the area of reestablishing ourselves.

Everywhere I have ever lived my entire life, the Lord has graciously and generously blessed me with friends. I do my small part of taking tiny, measurable action steps, but He always, *always* has just the right women He brings into my life for that particular season. He has always allowed me to be surrounded by a wonderful worship community. God has always provided leadership, volunteer, or employment opportunities no matter the state or city. I have to keep from getting ahead of myself and ahead of God. I can pull all the strings I want and make all of the moves, and host all of the get-togethers, but it is God who orchestrates my life. It is God who hand picks that circle of people whose hearts will knit together with mine.

What He Needed:

In our marriage, Ryan knows that I need external friendships. Where I consider myself an extroverted introvert, Ryan is a classic *introverted* introvert. As a chaplain and caregiver, Ryan often uses up all of his words and is emotionally depleted in a given day at work. When he gets home he needs quiet, solitude, and time to breathe in order to recharge his batteries.

Therefore, he appreciates those friends and communities that I can share with and who help to bear the burdens of my heart. Ryan also understands that as a homemaker, stay-at-home mom, and homeschooling mother of our three children, that I regularly need an outlet away from all of the daily operations of our home. That's not me being selfish. When I don't take the time to have other relationships outside of our immediate family, I can easily become a martyr. I can get overwhelmed and suffocated in the daily grind of wearing the mom/wife/teacher hat. Sometimes I just need to be able to wear the Claire hat.

While Ryan doesn't claim to need the outside friendships, encouragement, and empathy that friends give, he knows that I do. And to that end, he does everything in his power to accommodate my plans to regularly attend coffees, PWOC retreats, and Saturday breakfasts with my close circle. He sends me out for walks, encourages my participation in volunteer activities, blesses my time at Yoga classes at the YMCA and encourages time out for socializing with friends.

Where I need people to help recharge my batteries, Ryan needs time spent outside in nature to recharge his. Ryan is an avid outdoorsman and activities like deer hunting, turkey hunting, fishing, or playing golf help refresh and restore him. Just as he does all he can to accommodate my need for social interactions, I aim to cut him loose to be outside, alone, doing his thing too.

Ryan and I don't keep score anymore. It isn't about who gets to get out and do what he/she wants. In our marriage we aim to give the other the space that is needed at any given moment. We work really hard to accommodate schedules and plans in order for this to happen. I have to go out and search out the places and people I need when we get to a new duty station. Ryan has to study his topical maps and find the nearest water and hunting leases. To each his or her own!

There is a beautiful give-and-take in mission ready marriages. Ryan recognizes my needs and works toward helping me meet them. I recognize his and do the same. Our relationship functions best when each of us elevates the others' needs above our own. In turn, we each feel happier, more at peace, and more grateful for our spouse. The marriage bond is a steady, safe harbor when everything else surrounding us feels new and precarious.

From My Blog: "People of His Pasture"

I go through spells where I will not shed a tear for weeks or months. Then I go through spells where the tears flow freely. Lately it's been the latter. Most recently I have been crying when I see other people post pictures of taking their kids off to college on Facebook and Instagram. (Um, okay?) And I have been crying over decisions about planning next year's summer vacation. (Poor Ryan.) And I have been especially crying during times of hearing music; namely many of the hymns I've made into a playlist for our study this year and songs we are singing at church. (Poor everyone in my path.)

I used to be ashamed of my ability to cry at the drop of a hat. Seriously, there are moments when I literally have no control over the wetness leaving my tear ducts. I once cried over a very competitive game of Classic Concentration (Jamie?), trading, selling or buying a vehicle (Dad? Ryan?), and once driving through the city of Douglas, GA (Ryan). I used to think I was overly sensitive and emotional. And the older I've gotten, I don't just think it…I know it.

No longer do I make apologies for my tears, for feeling empathy or strong emotions of gratitude, sadness or a conflicted heart. For this I have come to realize; our tears are precious to Jesus.

I have written much here about the dryness and spiritually parched time I spent in the desert. I know the time we were in El Paso taught me much. I relied on God in a mighty way. He was my provision. As parched and depleted as I felt, there were still many tears during that season. It was a necessary and precious season to me. But even only a few months into our time in Georgia, I am noticing a theme already. If in Texas my faith felt dry, barren and desert-like, then Georgia is helping my faith to be built up as a green, verdant oasis.

Today, I meander through my backyard with my camera in hand trying to capture the essence of His creation and His majesty and His goodness. I see these giant trees and feel this amazing cool breeze and reflect on all of the many, many wonderful blessings God has provided in just two months since we landed in town and I am simply overwhelmed. It already feels like we are in a place of renewal and refreshment. From being nearer to family, to having found a wonderful, life-giving church and chapel, to barely budding friendships and relationships all around. These are all things I so desperately need; all things God so graciously provides.

The past several years of transitioning from civilian life to Army life has proven a giant exercise in obedience for me. Maybe it isn't so much a transition that is still in process as much as it is just learning to live and flourish in the life God has called you to. Maybe it's learning to live at the feet of the Great Shepherd. There's freedom in that after all. Everyone (military or not) is called to something. Each of us has to figure that out for ourselves. The conflict lies in our human nature wanting to have our own way and reconciling that to God's will. That is the eternal human struggle.

I am often an unruly sheep. But my God is a loving Shepherd who uses His rod and staff to protect and guide and teach discipline. Can I *choose to devote our family life to serving the military community even when it costs me some of my comforts? Can I be okay not knowing all of the details of my days? Am I at rest even when I feel alone and struggle to connect with friends? Human nature says no way! Human nature says revolt Flee! Go your own way! Escape! Figure it out on your own; take matters into your own hands!*

I have decided not to flee from or escape this journey God has our family on. Indeed, many days that seems logical and even desirable; especially on those days when I feel alone and lonely in a new place. Rather, I have committed myself to His plans and purposes no matter how many times I have to reset my heart and mind and remind myself that He is God, I am not. He is sovereign. He can be trusted. For He is good.

That is precisely where my tears meet me. In spite of life's difficulties and challenges, our God is there walking along side us, carrying us when necessary. In my gratitude for God allowing me to come before Him with great thanksgiving and requital, the overflow of my heart is tears.

In my tears I find grace. In my tears I find an unmerited, divine assistance given for my regeneration and sanctification. Both require time. Both require a process, a journey. Both require perspective. And for me, both occasionally require tears. Revival in my heart. Growth in my faith.

God's Use for the Trial:

I know that there is nothing wasted in our experiences. There is no change, no move, no loneliness, and no friendship that God can't use to bring about transformation in our lives. And while it may require patience on my end to wait for those new friendships, jobs, or connections, God and His presence is always available for me. God doesn't ask me to come looking for Him, searching out and seeking to find Him to no avail. He is ever present and offers me His constant comfort.

I think those of us who have dedicated our lives and marriages to serving our country have possibly an even deeper need to feel understood, known, and counted. Our lives come with some extra emotional baggage that our civilian friends and family members just can't understand or appreciate. The fellowship and connections in a new town helps us find our place where we fit and belong. It is there we can sometimes feel best appreciated with empathy and approval.

As much as I may value deep friendships, fellowship, a hobby or new job, I must work hard to maintain the proper place for these things in my life. It's easy for me to make an idol out of desperately needing to be understood and accepted in a new place. I know firsthand the important and integral roles these joys of life play for a military spouse. God desires that place in my heart above all else.

There is a balance in relying too much upon our friends or careers when God has given us wonderful spouses who love and support us. God must maintain first place, then our spouses and families next. Our various networks, while vital, should come third in that hierarchy. There have been days I have overlooked the blessings of the relationships in my own home as I've been preoccupied with establishing myself at our new assignment.

God longs for us to fellowship with Him and sit at His feet. I can whine and wallow in my frustrations about relocating and moving and feeling all of the emotions that come along with being new in town (again). Or I can choose to leave those burdens with Him and trade my yoke for His. When we are lonely or feeling like we could use another female shoulder to cry on or her nod to agree that this life isn't easy, we already have One Friend that will never leave or forsake us.

"Come to Me, all who labor and are heavy laden, and I will give you rest." {Matthew 11:28}

A mission ready marriage discerns the need for rest, care, & outside connections.

Questions for Reflection:

1. Among all of the many things that you have to do when you arrive at a new duty station, what ranks the highest as the thing you dislike the most? Is it something like finding a new place to get your hair cut? Or making new friends? Finding a good place for coffee? Learning your way around a new post or city?

2. Can you see why some people resort to just giving up on finding new friends each time they PCS? What would ever cause you to feel this way or finally throw in the towel on the often intimidating task of starting again with new relationships?

3. What are some of your go-to methods for making friends? Do you prefer to connect online through social media? In person? Do you scope out women's ministry opportunities? A new job? The gym? Unit events? Your neighbors?

4. Would you describe yourself as mostly introverted or extroverted or a combination of both? What do you typically look for most in a friend? What would you consider to be some of the unique things about yourself

that make you a good friend to others? What about your spouse? How do you see these personality differences and needs playing an important role in making your marriage stronger?

5. Is it difficult for you to rest in the fact that God has our cares in His best interest including details like our needs to feel connected when we move to a new duty station? Why or why not? What are some tangible ways you can trust Him more and let the process of meshing in your community unfold naturally?

Chapter 11

The Friendships of Women

From the time I was a young girl, I have always been drawn to the comforts of a good, trustworthy friend. From my elementary years when friends and I would make *"No boys allowed"* clubs to the later tumultuous years of junior high and high school, I relied on friendships to help me navigate the waters of each of life's seasons.

I love the mutual investment that is established when two women take the time, energy, and emotions to connect. Were it not for my dearest friends, I don't know how I would have made it through college boyfriend break ups, new jobs, being a clumsy newlywed, and those first monumental rites of passage as a new mother. There's much wisdom to be gleaned from a friend who has walked in your shoes months or years *ahead* of you, as well as a friend who is willing to walk *beside* you when life hands you challenges.

Friends will help throw you a wedding shower and stay up all night giggling about the nuances of having a new husband. Friends will visit you when you have your first baby and bring you extra diapers when they visit you with your third. Friends know that book club night or Bunco night is really just an excuse to get together and share our struggles and our hearts. Friends help you realize that you are not alone in this world. It's those times when we don't reach out to friends and don't allow another to embrace life's difficulties and joys with us, that we can feel isolated and like we are alone in our journey and in our pain. Worst of all when we don't reach out to friends, we may often feel that we unable to handle what life gives us.

I praise the Lord that He had already allowed me a lifetime of full, rich friendships and the knowledge that this brings, long before He set Ryan and me on this path into military service. I simply cannot imagine being thrown into this life without the skill set and life experiences that shaped me into a person who values and makes friends easily.

While I don't think it's absolutely necessary for each of us to go out deliberately seeking an official mentor, I do think there is something so profound and practical in having someone steps ahead of us holding our hand.

Back during the Christmas holiday when our family was doing our Advent devotions, we were daily working through Scripture reading and focusing on the coming of Christ. We methodically traced the Root of Jesse and followed the promise of a soon coming King through the lineage of Abraham, Ruth, and David all the way to the characters in the book of Luke.

What struck me for maybe the first time ever, when reading this chronology and the events leading up to Christ's birth, was a beautiful relationship God ordained in the lives of Mary and Elizabeth. We have all heard over the years about how Mary must have felt alone and afraid with this news of her mission to deliver the Son of Man. Mary was young. Joseph was likely frightened and quite possibly clueless about childbirth and child rearing.

But I began to think about Mary in a very practical way. I began to think about her as a young, unwed, pregnant woman. I began to think of the anxieties she must have felt, about her pregnancy hormones, and feeling so unsettled as she and Joseph began a new life together only months before giving birth. Yet even as Gabriel, the angel of the Lord, gave her the knowledge of her pregnancy, he also foretold of Elizabeth's conception of John the Baptist.

It's been speculated that Mary stayed with Zechariah and Elizabeth during about three months of her pregnancy. I imagine that the two pregnant women shared many stories, many hopes, many worries, and many day to day talks about what lay ahead with their sons. I find it so incredibly awesome that the God of the Universe crafted into the story of Mary's life a friend and mentor to have during the time of her pregnancy. Elizabeth delivered her son John ahead of Mary's delivery of Christ. How awesome for Mary to get to see how

Elizabeth dealt with her pregnancy, her delivery, and even her firm stance on naming John the Baptist, the prophet.

After this epiphany hit me, I began to think of all of the Elizabeths that I cherish. Who are those women who God ordained to be in my life as I have walked through major transitions? Where would I be without their guidance, support, and encouragement? These mothers (real and spiritual), these veteran spouses, these girlfriends, fellow sojourners on this road we're walking; these are the women who have held my hand and cheered the loudest.

Can you imagine if Elizabeth had been the kind of person in Mary's life that told her about how big her ankles were going to swell, how painful the hours of labor would be, how Joseph would probably snore right through nighttime feedings? What if Elizabeth consistently told Mary, "*Good luck, you're going to hate being the mother of the Son of God?*" What if all Elizabeth ever told Mary was how difficult being pregnant or being a mother would be? This would have made a world of difference in Mary's outlook and attitude, of course.

I learned about three days after we set foot at our first duty station that Negative Nancy and Debbie Downer had no place in my life. I didn't need to hear that military life was terrible, that marriages don't survive, and that my kids would turn out terribly all because Ryan had committed himself to military service. NO!

I quickly learned the importance of having as many Elizabeths in my life as possible. I needed the truth and reality, yes. But mostly I needed to hear the joys, the successes, and the triumphs of service. I needed to hear of the delights and blessings of what it means to put the love of God and country above self; of the benefits and victories of strong military marriages; of the successes and achievements of capable military children. I also began to realize just as much as I needed Elizabeths in my own life, how much more so did I need to be an Elizabeth to the other women God placed around me?

We all have bad days or moments where we need to vent and release negative emotions. No one expects fake perfection. However, I began to feel an immediate responsibility to let it never be said that I was a hater of this life. I made a vow to myself and Ryan that if it ever got to the point that I could no longer keep a cheerful and supportive attitude about our circumstances, then it would be time to hang up our hats.

What I Needed:

All of my life I have been blessed to have many positive
influences surrounding me. However, before we even arrived
at the doorstep of our first duty station, God had already
prepared the way. Just as He gave Mary the mentor in
Elizabeth, He graciously placed a handful of women in my
life who were walking a few (or many) steps ahead on this
military road.

God gave me Brenda as a model of a military spouse
who'd made it through her husband's career with her own
sanity, marriage, professional calling, and flourishing children
intact. God gave me Kelly to show me how important my
own faith is in this military life. Husbands and children bring
us great joy; but it is our strong and fervent prayer life and
time spent in the Word of God that sustains us.

God gave me Cathy to model for me the importance and
joy in standing and serving beside her husband in service to
our country and in God's kingdom. She helped me to
navigate the new roads of homeschooling as a former public
school teacher herself.

God gave me Ginger to show me that military life and
stress can take a physical toll if we don't care for ourselves.
She encouraged me by example to get rest, exercise, and care
when needed. Ginger modeled for me a strong presence in

unit leadership. She also taught me never, *never*, under any circumstances should you adopt a new pet during a deployment!

God gave me Tiffany as a wonderful example of finding your passions and pursuing them even when it is a complicated and time consuming process. Tiffany exemplifies that our gifts, our strengths, and our own talents matter. Marriage is a partnership and we each bring something of value to the relationship. That doesn't have to get lost as a military spouse.

God gave me Amy to model for me that life is meant to be lived fully, whether my husband is home or not. Trips and vacations shouldn't wait. Wonderful meals and fellowship are worth the investment. Life should not be suspended when our soldiers are away. We are all living an adventure and we can be adventurers together!

The Lord knew I needed to have these pictures of strength, joy, survival, gratitude and perseverance. I firmly believe that God is continually weaving different people into the fabric of our lives. He knows down to the tiniest details what kinds of friendships and women will uplift us and carry us through our highs and lows.

What He Needed:

I'm not sure Ryan would ever articulate that he, too, needs an Elizabeth in his life. However, I think men also generally benefit from mentor relationships. Thankfully, by the structure of the military, service members are naturally able to witness these type of leaders and examples in normal work settings. It's wise for all people, men included, to reflect upon the successes and qualities of those who rank ahead in their jobs. Ryan is able to witness the fibers of what makes a good chaplain by looking at the model and patterns of brigade, division, and garrison chaplains who go before him.

Men wouldn't dare admit the value of community, accountability, and friendship lest their man-cards be revoked, but it's true, we ALL need friendship. Men probably don't sit around gabbing and tearfully admitting their struggles, but maybe a nod, a grunt, or fist-bump between them delivers the same message. We all need the human acknowledgment toward another that says, "*I get it. I get you; I understand.*"

Ryan realizes that part of my makeup, is finding community with like-minded friends and spiritual sisters. He knows full well the benefits of me having a close circle of Godly women in my life to uplift and uphold; with whom to pray and study God's word together; to help shoulder the often heavy burdens of military life.

It is vital to our marriage that these relationships are nurtured. If not, I begin to misplace responsibility on Ryan's shoulders to meet the needs that only friends and mentors can meet in my life. Like the narrative of Mary and Elizabeth, there is no way in that Joseph could have been for Mary what she needed in Elizabeth. I would even go as far as to say that Mary was better for Joseph *because* of Elizabeth. Ultimately these relationships are God's gifts of grace to us and our marriages.

From My Blog: "Persevere"

I have always had a great network of friends, from church friends, mom friends, lifelong friends, work colleague friends, neighbor friends, friends from book club and Bunco, to elementary, high school, college and sorority friends. I have friends new and old. That's just my personality to find and make friends. But never in my life have I experienced the degree of friendship that I have seen in my Army sisters. I'm talking a whole new level here. These friends are the kind that don't even ask you what you need. They just do for you what you may not be able to do for yourself. No questions asked. No strings attached. And they don't just help you, they help everyone. If there's a need, there's someone to have your back.

I'm going to cry if I keep thinking about these friends. These friends make you meals, dry your tears, ease your anxiety, watch your kids, love your kids like their own, offer you rides, relax your burdens, hear you out, know your heart, and even help keep your gray-headed roots covered up. My final devotion as PWOC president sums it up best.

(April 24, 2013 PWOC Fort Bliss)

"I recently read a book, which incidentally it is a book shared with me by another Army wife, and its title is <u>Saving CeeCee Honeycutt</u> by Beth Hoffman. It is the story of 12 year old CeeCee in pre-Civil Rights Savannah, Georgia. CeeCee moved there after the tragic death of her mother. There are many characters in this story that 'fill in the gaps' of

CeeCee's new life. They are her Great Aunt Tootie, Tootie's house-help, Oletta, the elderly Mrs. O'Dell, the eccentric Miz Goodpepper, Thelma Rae and a new friend CeeCee's own age with whom she attends school.

CeeCee (like many of us) has been uprooted from the life she's always known and is forced to find her new position in a new city. Sounds all-too familiar, huh? One of my favorite quotations in this story is spoken by Oletta when she says, 'Life is full of change honey. That's how we learn and grow. When we're born, the Good Lord gives us each a Life Book. Chapter by chapter, we live and learn.' What I most took away from reading this book is that CeeCee, like many of us, is taken care of by not just one person, but an entire slew of women that come to her rescue. In essence, CeeCee lives the proverb, 'It takes a village.'

This is not a Christian book, but rather a secular fiction read--but its message left me feeling a close parallel to how I see PWOC functioning (this past year and in the future). Did you all know, besides the Four Aims of PWOC, there is actually also a Readiness Position Statement?

It reads: 'PWOC as part of the religious program is to minister to the unique needs of the military woman and female military spouse. PWOC equips women to FLOURISH in the UNIQUE CHALLENGES of the military lifestyle through its emphasis on NURTURING and MENTORING.'

Nurturing calls to check on a sister who has been M.I.A. (missing in action) through setting up Meal Trains and taking meals when there's a new baby or surgery. Nurturing trades out babysitting with a tired mama, pitching in for Watchcare needs so no one bears that burden alone. Nurturing brings snacks to her class, sends a beautiful hand-drawn and illustrated card just because. Nurturing treats a friend to a birthday lunch or says 'Sure, I can pick you up' or 'Yes, you can hitch a ride to the retreat with me.' Nurturing drags you around the track or pushes you to hit the gym to burn off some stress. Nurturing delivers leftovers to your doorstep when you know cooking is the last thing you can handle.

Nurturing messages you the day your husband leaves for training or a deployment and says 'Let's hang out in our sweat pants, eat ice cream and cry together.' Nurturing offers you some cast-off household goods that she can't take with her overseas on her next PCS. Nurturing opens up her home to you and your family for Thanksgivings and Christmases that are too far away to travel home. Nurturing gives you rides to and from the airport, keeps an eye out on your house while you travel, has keys to your house and knows the security code. Nurturing sits in (literally) as your 'church pew husband' during separations. Nurturing insists on bringing Gatorade and Lysol when your kids get the stomach virus. Nurturing keeps your kids so you can go to the gynecologist/ chiropractor/hair salon/commissary alone. Nurturing fundraises for your adoption and offers to wash laundry when you travel home from India.

Nurturing prays and awaits with you for test results, orders, good news and blackouts. Nurturing wraps her loving arms around a sister, who, through tears is struggling to get through a meaningful praise and worship song. Nurturing shares books, movies, recipes, White Sands sleds, vehicles, ice cream makers, cupcake stands and homeschooling wisdom. Nurturing comes early and stays late; it comforts a newborn during a Bible study to give a new mom a free hand to open up the Word; it empties trash cans, brings donuts, returns name tags, washes dishes. Nurturing asks 'How can I help?' or says 'You're special' or 'I completely understand' or at worst, 'I am so sorry.' Nurturing helps the needy both among us and within our city; it donates its time, its treasures and its talents. Nurturing embraces its arms around you, stands with you, prays for you and sends you on with a blessing. And lastly, nurturing is that friend who senses that you just might need a smile, an encouraging word, a hug, some chocolate or flowers and she senses this maybe even before you know it!

I love the passage of Scripture found in Matthew 6:8 that simply says, 'Your Heavenly Father knows what you need before you even ask...' God knew that every one of us would need all of those things on that laundry list I just mentioned (all of which are actual events witnessed this year) and God in His infinite wisdom ordained these women in this room (and beyond these walls) for such a time as this...here in El Paso, Texas...at Fort Bliss...way out in the desert.

The Bible says in Ecclesiastes 4:9-12 that, 'Two are better than one, because they have a good return for their labor; If either of them falls down, one can help the other up...' Just like all of the women placed around the fictional character of CeeCee Honeycutt, God has surrounded each of us with our PWOC sisters for the chapter of our Life Book called Fort Bliss. These women in the story were young and old and of all ages and stages in between.

This brings me to the second part of that Readiness Position Statement, 'MENTORING.' This year, our International Theme has been Generation to Generation. What a divinely appointed, timely theme to address mentoring. Psalm 145:4 (our theme verse) says, 'One generation commends (or praises) Your works to another; they tell of Your mighty acts...'

It is through our relationships that we share our testimonies, His power through the bonding at Sacramento (retreat center), through our brainstorming at board meetings, through shared praise and worship, through the ways we've all opened up and been transparent in our studies each semester, through the devotions shared by Lori N., Lori J., Krista, Sarah, Corie, Ginger J., Cathy, Betsey and others. These generations have declared all of the ways God has brought them through the trials of life and carried each of them in His loving, gracious hands. His hands that offer peace, consolation, and sustainment of the highest order.

When we mentor, it isn't simply an older woman being paired up with another (younger) woman for wisdom to be imparted...although it can happen in that way. Mentoring can simply mean that when we mentor one another, we serve as a tutor, guide, coach or cheerleader. It happens when, like Philippians 2:14 says, 'Therefore if you have any encouragement from being united with Christ, if any comfort from His love, if any common sharing in the Spirit, if any tenderness and compassion, then make my Joy complete by being like-minded, having the same love, being in one Spirit and of one mind. Do nothing out of selfish ambition or vain conceit. Rather, in humility value others above yourselves, not looking to your own interests but each of you to the interests of others...'

So to each of you in this room (and those who are here in spirit as we have already said, 'See you later' earlier this year), I want to say thank you! Thank you for first loving the One, True, Living God. Thank you for serving Jesus Christ in word and deed. Thank you for being here for each other, with no demands, no drama...only your desire to grow in love. Thank you for being the 'iron that sharpens iron...' Thank you for filling in the gaps, for serving, for nurturing each other, for being mentors, coaches, tour guides along this ever-adventurous Army-journey.

Thank you for being the Olettas, the Mrs. O'Dells, the Aunt Tooties, and the Miz Goodpeppers to each other and to me. Thank you for being who you are and allowing the sisters sitting all around you to FLOURISH. May your names be written in one another's Life Books as you serve as tangible reminders of the characters the Lord has placed in this chapter.

God's Use for the Trial:

Although many of us may not always recognize our need for the comforts only friendships can offer, it's imperative that we give credence to that necessity. I firmly believe that God allowed me over three decades of interacting favorably with an array of friendships, to groom my personality for life in the military. I also know that whether you are a natural friend maker or maybe just reluctantly friendly in new settings, with God's help you can build wonderful relationships with Godly women.

I imagine if you just begin to look around you there are already women in your circle with whom you can find common interests, invest in meaningful discussions and conversations, and grow in your spiritual maturity. God doesn't intend for us to walk through this life alone, struggling to make sense of our current situations. He gives grace and wisdom to those who seek it. So often that wisdom can be found in a woman, like the Biblical Elizabeth, who is a season ahead of our own life.

It's important to recognize that the company we keep can define our entire outlook and viewpoint of life. The friends we associate with are a direct forecast to whether we see our lives and choices in a positive or negative light.

Having wise mentors and friends who champion and cheer on our causes helps us to foster a better view of ourselves, our faith, and our marriage. In a life of active duty service, there is really no way to survive and enjoy this life if you don't let anyone in. Having an openness toward friendship and willingness to learn rich lessons of experience can help make us better spouses and partners.

"Whoever walks with the wise becomes wise, but the companion of fools will suffer harm." {Proverbs 13:20}

A mission ready marriage highly regards the wisdom and influence of mentors and guides.

Questions for Reflection:

1. Describe the theme of friendship in your life. Have you typically surrounded yourself with good friends or have the friends you've kept had an unsound impact on your life?

2. Has there been a particular friendship that has impacted you in a profound way? Was this a positive experience and if so, what good came of the friendship? Did associating with this person have an adverse impact upon your own attitude or actions?

3. What do you think of this idea that God knew Mary would need a mentor in Elizabeth? Can you find any other nuances of their friendship that would translate into modern day friendship?

4. Right this moment, are there any Elizabeths in your life? Do you have regular contact with these women? In what setting? Are you observing them from afar or do you openly discuss the *mentor/mentee* relationship? What do you see in being the greatest value in these friendships?

5. Much like the CeeCee Honeycutt excerpt I shared from my blog and devotional, do you agree that it "takes a village" and a variety of women, living life in various stages/ seasons to help us along? Name at least three people that you would say you'd include in your "Life Book."

Chapter 12

The "S" Word and Other Profanities

I'm not much of a cusser. I never really have been. Sure, I've let a few swears slip over the years, but using bad words has never been a thing for me. So much so, that it frequently catches me off guard to be around people who drop those verbal bombs during the course of pedantic conversations.

I remember the first time I saw one of those frequently posted signs on a military installation. Nearly all of the entry points had signs posted that shared a *"No Profanity"* message as these areas were family friendly. Our family had come to check out the Freedom Crossing area at Fort Bliss where the commissary, food court, and post exchange are all housed.

Initial naive questions of *"Why would the Army need to post those signs"* filled my mind? But it didn't take long until I realized that the military bred a culture where curse words were just a way of life. The more swearing a person could fit into a given conversation, the tougher and more hard core he/she appeared. Ryan even warned me to not be too offended. After his three month stint in training on another post, he knew that hearing profane words was about as common as seeing green uniforms.

As a Believer in Christ, there is a word in our culture that often carries a negative connotation. This word is so full of meaning and varying degrees of implication that to many, it, too, is a curse word. The word I am talking about is the "S" word, *submission*. The major context in which this word was discussed is found in the passage of Scripture in Ephesians, chapter 5. We are given the mandate *"Wives submit to your own husbands as unto the Lord."* The words that follow, *"for the husband is the head of the wife..."* and we wince and writhe and for some of us the hairs on our necks prickle up.

For many people, even Believers, our ideas about submission stop there. We quickly form strong opinions in this post-modern, feminist age that women should rise up against the perceived oppression of men, that men are not superiors, bosses or lords over women. The entire intent of that Biblical mandate can get lost in society's ideologies before Scriptural accuracy is ever fully understood. The Bible doesn't tell us to lie down like doormats and let our husbands rule us. If we continue reading that passage we see that there is much mutual submission by the husband in God's economy. If we are living a Godly, Biblical model of marriage, both husband and wife are laying aside self and submitting their needs and desires to the other person. Submission isn't a bad word, it's a word of freedom!

What's more is that God gives us an Earthly relationship in marriage to model the spiritual relationship He longs to have with all of His children, regardless of their gender. How much further, then, is that metaphor lived out for those of us who submit our lives to the needs and desires of the United States government via our military service?

Quite literally, to submit means *"to give over or yield to the power or authority of another."* As human beings, that is one of the most difficult missions we will ever encounter. Our flesh often prevents us from easily setting aside our own wants, our own feelings of control and power to vulnerably and openly agree to the authority of another.

It's true, many of us hear the word submission and we panic. We retreat. We think about running. None of us particularly wants to cede control of our own lives to another. Even in the best of circumstances, it's difficult to trust that someone else may have our best interests in mind. It's difficult, even with the best spouse in the world, to fully believe that our needs and passions could come first or be elevated above his own.

Marriage is a great teacher. Being married to someone shows us the problems and the pains of our humanity. Being married shows us where we need improvement, where we need to die to self, where our narcissism and ego trips need to buried. Although a Biblical idea, the practice of submission is not just important for Christian marriages. Mutual submission is a good practice to follow in *all* marriages.

Submitting to Ryan doesn't mean that I have no opinions, no voice, and no value. Ryan submitting to me doesn't mean that I boss him around or turn him into a docile, browbeaten husband. Joint submission is about give and take. It looks out for the needs of the other above our own. It is founded in selflessness, service, forgiveness, and unconditional love.

God can use marriage to refine us in a way that no other relationship can. It has been through the ups and downs, and the ebbing and flowing in my own marriage that I have been able to see the greater good in submission.

Consider the organization of the military. How often do our service members submit applications, paperwork, forms, plans, wish lists, and approvals to their superiors? All the time. Submission is at the very core of the staff work done in the military. Zoom out that same lens a little farther. Think about the sacrifices and calling of being a soldier, airman, or marine. The very nature of a service member's duty is to lay down his/her life for another in submission or compliance with the wishes and orders of a superior. The job, the mission, and the tactical objective always comes first.

Those in the military are purposefully trained to set aside personal wants, plans, or even ideas. Military professionals follow orders and remove personal desire out of the equation. Most soldiers don't get paid for their bright ideas or innovation; most earn their paycheck by dutifully fulfilling the orders of those who outrank them.

Life in the Army can often be a daily liturgy in the observance of submission. I literally get no say in where I live, when I move, or how often I'll have the same address. I have a continual right to yield over the power and authority in my life to the hands of Uncle Sam. True, he may or may not have my own best interests at heart, but because I serve a loving God, I know that the ultimate submission to Him makes my subjection and obedience to my husband and the Army all the more possible.

Oh if only it were that easy in our spiritual lives. If only we were able to objectively set aside our ideas and intentions and simply allow the orders God gives us in His Word to guide us. If only we were capable of just laying aside self for the enduring promises of the life God wants for us.

What I Needed:

I've always been a very openly opinionated woman. Even as a child I held a strong viewpoint on just about anything a person might ask me about. Through my dating years I was never one to let a guy strong arm me out of my deep convictions whether about physical boundaries, ideas of my worldview, or even my theological beliefs. I may have often used words to describe myself as independent, bossy, a know-it-all, and self-reliant.

The first few years of our marriage were a lesson in humility. Two people living in the same household sharing the highs and lows of each day will quickly show a person's true colors. There were countless moments of stubbornness, selfishness, stinginess, and overt personal indulgence. And that was just ME!

Those descriptions all point to a sinful, human nature that wants its own way. I have to fight those tendencies to submit my strong will to the will of God. I have to die to those fleshly desires for control, for being right, and for thinking I have all of the answers. I regularly have to confess those faults to God and ask Him to replace the ugly parts of me with His goodness and holiness.

Thankfully, the Lord is at work in my life and continues to work in our marriage. Ryan and I are learning to live out our marriage in mutual submission to one another. When we submit to the truth of God's Word in our own lives, it becomes easier to submit in our marriage too. As our years of military service are rolling along these familiar pathways of practicing acquiescence to a greater Authority has made all the difference.

Do I still go kicking and screaming when the Army gets it wrong, doesn't ask my opinion or makes a big, life altering decision for me? You bet. Do I still have moments where my fleshly desires loom large and want their own way? Often.

But I am learning that the ride is so much smoother when I can set aside what I want and what I think may be best and just rest and relish in the good plans that the Lord has for me and the good thoughts He thinks toward me.

What He Needed:

As has routinely been the case, Ryan learned these lessons of surrender and submission light years ahead of me. Ryan in his patience, wisdom, observant and reflective nature has held the key to much lifelong happiness for quite some time. Ryan is a man who is confident in who he is as a child of God. He's also keenly aware of who God is. Ryan recognizes the power and knowledge of the God we serve and therefore knows his place as a small fish in God's big ocean.

It has been easy, for the most part for Ryan to honor me in mutual submission in our marriage. In kind, he has made an easy transition into military life where there's a definite pecking order and his job is to lead by following, to be strong in meekness, and to guide by yielding.

Ryan can easily look to God's master plan and love for us in every decision and mandate the military throws our way. Called to minister to soldiers? The Army and a selection board didn't decide that, God did. Sent to Fort Bliss in El Paso, Texas and Fort Gordon in Augusta, Georgia? His branch manager and the assignment board didn't fully decide that, God did. God sends us where HE wants us, where HE can use us best. Ryan sees the big picture and is able to draw strength and peace from it continually. I frequently suffer from spiritual amnesia.

From My Blog: "There's Been a Death in Our Marriage"

For the past three years, Ryan and I have been separated on our anniversary. In 2011 he was finishing his chaplain officer training in South Carolina. In 2012, he was at Fort Irwin, California doing a grueling training for pre-deployment and last year, in 2013, he was winding down his time in Afghanistan. For the past year, we have been adamant about planning something for our anniversary. With the Army, you never know if you'll get to be together and this year in 2014, while we are together, a trip was going to happen! What follows may be the most dispiriting anniversary message ever.

Over the summer I have been digging into C.S. Lewis's _Mere Christianity_ a little deeper and a few weeks ago, I came across a passage that I just couldn't get off my mind. As our anniversary of 13 years of marriage approached, I knew that I wanted to include a portion of that passage in a card/letter to Ryan.

{C. S. Lewis, _Mere Christianity_}

"What we call 'being in love' is a glorious state, and, in several ways, good for us. It helps to make us generous and courageous, it opens our eyes not only to the beauty of the beloved but to all beauty, and its subordinates (especially at first) our merely animal sexuality; in that sense, love is the great conqueror of lust. No one in his senses would deny that being in love is far better than either common sensuality or cold self-centeredness. But, as I said before, 'the most dangerous thing you can do is to take any one impulse of

241

our own nature and set it up as the thing you ought to follow at all costs.' Being in love is a good thing, but it is not the best thing. There are many things below it, but there are also things above it. You cannot make it the basis of a whole life. It is a noble feeling, but it is still a feeling. Now no feeling can be relied on to last in its full intensity, or even to last at all. Knowledge can last, principles can last, habits can last; but feelings come and go. And in fact, whatever people say, the state called 'being in love' usually does not last. If the old fairy tale ending 'They lived happily every after' is taken to mean 'They felt for the next fifty years exactly as they felt the day before they were married,' then it says what probably never was nor ever would be true, and would be highly undesirable if it were. Who could bear to live in that excitement for even five years? What would become of your work, your appetite, your sleep, your friendships? But, of course, ceasing to be 'in love' need not mean ceasing to love. Love in this second sense--love as distinct from 'being in love' --is not merely a feeling. It is a deep unity, maintained by the will and deliberately strengthened by habit; reinforced by (in Christian marriages) the grace which both partners ask, and receive, from God. They can have this love for each other even at those moments when they do not like each other; as you love yourself even when you do not like yourself. They can retain this love even when each would easily, if they allowed themselves, to be 'in love' with someone else. 'Being in love' first moved them to promise fidelity: this quieter love enables them to keep the promise. It is on this love that the engine of marriage is run: being in love was the explosion that started it. {...} The sort of thrill a boy has at the first idea of flying will not go on when he has joined the R.A.F. and is really learning to fly. The thrill you feel on first seeing some delightful place dies away when you really go live there. Does this mean it would be better not to learn to fly and not to live in the beautiful place? By no means. In both cases, if you go through with it, the dying away of the first thrill will be compensated by a quieter and more lasting kind of interest. What is more (and I can hardly find words to tell you how important I think this), it is just the people who are ready to submit to the loss of the thrill and settle down to the sober interest, who are then most likely to meet new thrills in some quite different direction. The man who has learned to fly and become a good pilot will suddenly discover music; the man who has settled down to live in the beauty spot will discover gardening. This is, I think, one little part of what Christ meant by saying that a thing will not really live unless it first dies. It is simply no good trying to keep any thrill: that is the very worst thing you can do. Let the thrill go---let it die away--- go on through that period of death into the quieter interest and happiness that follow---and you will find you are living in a world of new thrills all the time."

Ryan and I have joked all weekend about how (not) uplifting that message of Lewis's sounds upon first thought. But after you really digest the message, I think it's simply beautiful. Being in love does not last. Feelings come and go. Isn't that just the truth of it? Romantic get-aways are great. Nice dinners out are wonderful. Date nights are a must. Keeping the flame alive, totally worth it! But the day-to-day living, the habits, the will and the grace is where the rubber meets the road.

It's Ryan setting the coffee pot every night before bed and me making his lunch for work. It's Ryan filling my vehicle with gas before he gets back to the house and me keeping him stocked in his favorite toilet paper. It's Ryan spending hours shopping for antiques and me spending hours on a Jonboat hoping that he catches a few fish.

And it is here, where we find ourselves now. After thirteen years, we both know the habit and customs of the liturgy and litany of submission. We both know the benefit of settling down to common and individual sober interests. And most beautifully, we are meeting new thrills in many, varied directions. (Two cross-country moves in three years, anyone?)

Marriage is tricky. It is human nature to want to seek and serve yourself. It's natural to look out for our own best interests. Score-keeping, grudge-holding, and line-drawing in the sand is commonplace. In doing so, we keep self at the center of our universe. That's why there must be a certain death to self; a dying off of what I want, what I need, what I feel, what I choose in order to elevate the wants, needs, feelings and choices of the other. And it isn't just me dying to myself on Ryan's behalf. It's a mutual death, and includes him squelching out his "self" on my behalf as well.

Let me be clear, we have not achieved this. This dying must be daily. Life's ebbs and flows (and dare I say pre-menopausal hormones) make this an act of the will and a daily choice among us. We have NOT arrived, but after 13 years, I am happy to say that we have at least recognized the importance of laying aside self for the other. The world says, chase the thrill. The world says, live for number one. The world says, trust your feelings and do what feels good.

The world says, if my husband or wife isn't giving me what I need or want, it's okay to look somewhere else. The world says, if my husband or wife isn't satisfying me, I can look for that satisfaction elsewhere. The world says, chase what you want...where you want...when you want. I needed the reminder from C.S. Lewis that even when we feel that our marriage may look different from what we see around us, knowing that "a thing will not really live unless it first dies" is really what we are chasing after when we're seeking to live a life kneeling toward the cross of Christ. I am so grateful that we have had the opportunity and years and experiences to know that letting some of the thrill go means that we are on our way to the "quieter interest and happiness that follows." And that through our mutual submission (not just to each other, but to the life Christ has called us to) that we are really and truly "living in a world of new thrills all the time."

It was such a blessing to Ryan and me to have this weekend to reflect on all of the living that we have done in the past 13 years. It was equally exciting to look ahead to the next 13 years and beyond to dream about all of the possibilities; both known and unknown. We say so often that we really didn't know each other at all, those many years ago at the altar, making a vow and covenant before God and 300 witnesses. We couldn't have known. We were simply "in love...generous and courageous." We were high on each other, high on life and full of an overwhelming desire to start a new thing together with the hope and promise of happiness.

Ryan, over a decade later, I am still full of hope and happiness and I am now looking forward to many, many more years of "settling down into sober interests," and "meeting [many] new thrills in quite different direction[s]."

God's Use for the Trial:

There's no better lifestyle than that of a family serving on active duty military service to illustrate this idea of submission. I look at the life God has given me, Ryan, and our children and feel extremely blessed that He thought enough of us to put us in this place of influence, of ministry, and of learning.

God doesn't make mistakes. He didn't choose the wrong family when He ordained this path for your family either. God knew that life as a military spouse would draw you unto Him. It would keep you focused on Christ and your utter need and dependence on Him.

Life in general demands that we see the smallness of ourselves in relationship to a big, all-powerful and holy God. Life in the military is that viewpoint honed in to a very fine degree. It's the more focused, succinct version of a life of smallness in regard to God's bigness. It's a life of blessing in the battle; joy in the journey; abundance in the absence of answers.

There are many days I don't think I am going to survive it; many weeks I'll think, "*Surely there is another job, another ministry, another calling my husband could have.*" I will whine and let my fleshly attitude rear its head and think "*Why can't my husband have one of those safe, nice 9-5 jobs where he never travels or is in harm's way?"* Or I think, *"Why can't we have a calling that keeps us in one place, near our friends and family so we aren't constantly uprooting and replanting?"*

I am always reminded that in a spiritual sense, we didn't choose this life. God hand-picked it for us. And I'll walk in the path of His commands any day over choosing what I think is best. I am choosing to submit my ways to embrace His. I've learned that *submission* is no longer a profanity or obscenity. Submission really makes my life much easier and my heart more content when I open myself up to its possibilities and potential.

"I delight to do Your will, O my God; Your law is within my heart." {Psalm 40:8}

A mission ready marriage submits to each other, to God, & to country.

Questions for Reflection:

1. Does the "S" word, *submission,* make you cringe? Why or why not? In what ways has the world made it an ugly word?

2. If you took a very personal, honest look into your marriage, how would you characterize the submission that takes place there? Is it one-sided? Mutual? God honoring?

3. Can you think of some ways unique to military families that we live lives of submission? Is this submission to the power or authority of our government difficult to live out?

4. Like C.S. Lewis advocates, what would you say are some of the greatest benefits of dying to self? How does this translate in general? As a wife? As a military spouse?

5. If you could focus on one area of your life in particular, where you'd like to see some change and work on strengthening your "submission" muscles, what area would it be? With a friend? Your husband? Your children? Extended family? Your attitude toward your military involvement?

Chapter 13

He Gives Us What We Need

When we are open to the idea of submission in one area of our lives, it tends to make us more receptive to submission in *every* area of our lives. When I am able to surrender my will to God's will, I can more easily accept my role alongside my husband serving our country. So what does that submission look like? Behind a life of submission are the ideas that we must first be *sanctified* and we are sanctified by that which is *sacred* in our lives.

I'll be honest here, sanctification is a churchy word that is often misunderstood and left alone. Many of us, myself included, often don't want to get our lives too messy, too mixed up, too bare, accessible, and defenseless to delve into what it means for Christ to sanctify us. We're too tired, too busy, and too stressed to even think about undergoing a process that could take years or even decades to come to fruition.

There's an often quoted catch phrase that I have heard Christians use. *"God's desire isn't to make us happy, it is to make us holy."* It sounds trite, but alas, it's certainly true. At the heart of the meaning of the word *sanctification* is this idea that as Christ followers we are consecrated, set apart for His purpose and use, free to pursue of a life of purity and holiness, free from sin.

Does God love me? Yes. Does He want to give me the desires of my heart? Possibly. Does He want me to live a life of happiness? That's a question I have misunderstood myself these first few years of military service. I assumed God wanted me happy but I have often mistaken happiness for a deeper-seated joy and contentment. Happiness can be fleeting, especially in a setting of constant change and uprooting. Walking faithfully in the mission to which God has called me brings joy even in these trials and pain.

I believe God truly does want to give me the desires of my heart when they align with His desires. He wants my heart *to want* the things that He wants of me. I think He wants my heart to desire the living fruit of his Holy Spirit (love, joy peace, patience, kindness, goodness, faithfulness, gentleness, self-control) *more* than to desire living near my family, getting to choose where I live, smooth transitions for my children, and constant meaningful friendships. Sanctification aligns my heart with God's, changing my desires, sometimes slowly, to match His.

The question is, *"Am I willing to allow Him to change my desires?"* Will I make the sacrifice of self that sanctification asks of me? The amazing reality is that God is not asking me to do anything that He has not already done. His love is sacrificial. God sacrificed Jesus, His Son, on the cross offering me the opportunity to know Him intimately. By following in His example of sacrifice, I am able to submit my will and ultimately my desires to be transformed by His grace.

Whether we serve our country for fifteen more years or five more minutes, I want to allow God to do this difficult work on my heart that it needs daily. I want Him to cut away the selfishness, the conceit, the jealousy, the doubt, and my constant impatience with His careful, loving scalpel. I want to be sanctified, purified, and refined through the fires of the trials He places in my path. When the work of the Spirit is active and alive in me, it cuts away at my selfishness and sin. Sanctification renews me and reminds me that God wants to use me the way He sees fit and the way He intends.

In the process of daily sanctification I witness God's work in my life. For a long time I thought that what I offered to God was sacred. I thought the sacrifices of my own comforts, the self-diagnosed martyrdom this military lifestyle requires, were those sacred things *I was giving back to God.* On this journey, I discovered that what *He gives me* through His mercy and grace becomes sacred to me. And more importantly, I discovered that the *means* through which He gives it is what is truly sacred.

God invites us to actively participate in the ongoing process of sanctification. The means through which that happens: faith exercised through prayer and confession, the reading of Holy Scripture, communion, fellowship and

Christian community, and as you might have guessed by now, through marriage. Marriage is the most sacred human relationship the Lord gives us to help demonstrate His love. It reflects the sacred relationship that Christ has with His followers. We have mission ready marriages when we serve one another, submit ourselves to our spouses, and when we offer grace to one another through the most difficult of seasons like deployments, reintegrations, and relocations.

As I look back, the past four years have provided varied experiences and trials. Despite my own weakness, I have still observed God at work in my life. Often times I didn't acknowledge those blessings in the moment but through the process of looking back with an attitude of thanksgiving, I see His fingerprints everywhere. I want to continually evaluate this one life I've been given and willingly submit to the sanctifying process of pruning away that God uses. I hope to take full advantage of those sacramental blessings as I consider that looming, larger narrative my Author, God is writing for me. He is composing a beautiful and meaningful story for my life. He is doing the same in your life too.

What I Needed:

The greatest thing I have needed over the past four years was to learn this lesson on my role and identity as a military spouse. I have felt utterly confused and unsure of where I fit into the picture. At times I have lacked patience and wisdom. At times I have just crumbled out of fear, frustration, and exhaustion from working so hard to win the approval of others. I wanted to feel settled and validated.

I felt for too long that I needed to know what I was supposed to do to be a proper military spouse. I wanted a formula, something predictable that I could control; a checklist I could mark off. I'd ask myself, *"What are the qualities of a vibrant, fulfilled, and flourishing military spouse and what does she look like?"* And I haven't known. I needed to realize that God has called me to love and honor Him in every faithful act I do and in every trusting step I take.

I needed to realize that despite an official job or title, I have an identity in Him. Christ sanctifies me and He alone establishes my path. Sometimes as military spouses we may see ourselves as small and insignificant in relationship to the great, patriotic jobs of our soldiers. We are often in the shadows, doing the small, mundane tasks that keep our marriages and our families afloat. To God, those jobs are not small, inconsequential, or meager. To God, those behind-the-scenes, behind-closed-doors, reverent and regarded works are the very offerings that are special to Him. He sees what we do as military spouses and recognizes that sometimes, despite isolation and a lack of identity in and of ourselves, we are honoring God's call in our lives.

Ultimately, I needed to say *"Here I am Lord. I am open and available. Use me how You see fit. Here I am Lord. Make me more aware of You. Here I am Lord, take whatever measures are necessary to make me more like You. Here I am Lord. I will continue to seek Your presence in my life."*

What He Needed:

Ryan has never asked of or expected perfection of me. Thank goodness! Sometimes I feel like I have failed him repeatedly over the years of our marriage. I'm not proud of these moments but after the fact, there isn't much I can do to change the outcome of certain events.

What I *can* do is continue to walk in willingness toward God's sanctification process in my own life. What I *can* do is continue recognizing the work God is doing all around me, in His grace, as sacred and precious which then leads to many positive outcomes in our marriage.

Ryan needs a wife that can walk confidently in the role God has placed before her. It removes a lot of pressure from him when I can let him be just Ryan, my husband and partner. He needs the freedom from my expectations that he will fulfill all of my needs and desires himself. He needs to know that I don't hold him accountable and responsible for all of my frustrations with military life. He needs to know that my own spiritual lamp isn't flickering. He needs my flame to stand brightly and chances are, your spouse needs much the same from you.

Whether in a truly theological sense of the word or just in a general sense, we all need the reminder that we are not called to "save" our spouses, or they, us. Saving work is God's work. All God asks of any of us is to walk in fellowship with Him. How freeing is that?

Imagine the possibilities in your own marriage if you were able to walk abundantly and confidently in the calling and identity God has for you! Imagine if you were so attuned to the sanctifying work of Christ that you recognized His handiwork and handprints everywhere you looked. Imagine if you were able to recognize and even find a precious appreciation for the sacred blessings He has designed uniquely and specifically just for you! That's not the role of a spouse. That's the role of a Savior.

From My Blog: "Identity"

Recently I had to go to the DEERS office on post to relinquish my soon-to-expire military ID card. I brought along a second form of photo identification, my power of attorney and a hopeful attitude that the whole process would be quick and painless. (Two words rarely associated with any office on a military installation!) To my great delight, there were no soldiers or other patrons waiting so I literally walked in and had my new ID card made. Ten minutes later I walked out still in a good mood.

As I'm prone to do, I remembered back to the day I drove down to the National Guard Armory in Chattanooga to get my first ID card made. Ryan had barely been commissioned and had yet to leave for his first training and we hadn't moved out of our old house and away from our old life just yet. There was much to learn about military life and so many new experiences awaiting us that I could have never dreamed up even if I tried. Little did I know the power of that card.

Now many years (many more gray hairs, more bags under my eyes, and several extra pounds) later, I have a new ID card and a much different outlook on what this little plastic card really is in the life of a military spouse. The ID card is everything in the life of a military spouse. It gets you on post, it gives you access to your healthcare, your benefits like using the commissary and may even offer you discounts around town. To the Army, as the spouse or dependent, I am basically nothing without my sponsor/soldier. This is a sobering, frustrating and *humbling thought. At times it has been a struggle for me trying to figure out who I am and where my place is in military life.*

My roles and relationships shift and change. Just as I may get comfortable wearing one hat, things change and it's time to figure out my role in that new set of circumstances. For many years, I found part of my identity in my profession as a teacher. I have found much of my identity in my friendships and my ability to be a friend. I have found my identity in my marriage and as a mother. I have found my identity in the places I have made my home.

As life ebbs and flows (and as the military life demands), many pieces of our identity come and go as well. I am learning that saying goodbye to parts of yourself can often be a slow, but painful process. Days, months or even years go by before you realize what has been robbed ever-so-gently by the thief of time. Friends that once held a close place in your heart have faded away. Passions you once had haven't had an opportunity to thrive so they, too, dim and tarnish. Sometimes that's part of the pruning process God intends for our good.

Getting my new ID card was an opportunity for personal reflection. Just as I realize that little pieces of who I am seem to come and go, ultimately, I was reminded that my true identity isn't found in Ryan, my children, friendships, the Army or in pursuing any of my passions. My identity can only be found in Christ. On the days when military life feels difficult or hard, or the days feel isolating or lonely, I have to be reminded of this very fact. I am God's chosen daughter; His own chosen child. He loves me at my best and at my worst.

My identity in HIM grants me access to far more benefits than MWR activities, discounted groceries and decent healthcare. My identity in HIM is greater than any earthly pursuit or relationship could ever yield. My identity in HIM has no bearing on whether I am a good teacher, friend, mother or wife and how I hope others see me.

My identity in Christ offers me a hope and a future no matter what the Army dictates. My identity in Christ offers me joy and gladness when I can't seem to see the silver lining. My identity in Christ offers me renewal, rebirth and sanctification, freeing me from a life of sin and death. Every time I pull this new card out of my wallet to gain access inside the gates of the installation or use it to get my 10% off at Lowe's or Sonic, I am going to be reminded that while thankful for my "privileges," that foremost, I am a child of God.

The life He has called me to in this season is that of a military spouse and supporter of my husband and the U.S. Army. Knowing who I am in Christ allows me the grace to perform my roles dutifully and with greater joy.

God's Use for the Trial:

   While I don't consider my entire life for the past four
years to be one giant trial, I can say that there have been some
constant and steady seasons where I have needed to exercise
some definite perseverance. It has been through my
indoctrination into Army life that God has been able to use
circumstances to teach me an utter and total dependence on
Him.

   I firmly believe that without the forced growth that has
taken place I would not be able to fully recognize just where
God has been all along in this process. For most of my life, I
had misplaced much of my security in my relationship with
my parents and extended family. I had unfairly placed too
much responsibility on Ryan's shoulders (and even my
children) to define and dictate my happiness. I had even
mistakenly allowed the Army permission to determine my joy
or sadness in my geographical location, my friendships, and
my role in our service.

   God has used this time to realign and readjust my
viewpoint and my heart. If for no other reason than this, I
know that my time as an active duty wife has rendered a
beautiful lesson. No person, thing, or organization will ever
satisfy me like Christ will. And although I have articulated
that idea here, in my humanity, I know it is an ongoing

reminder I must keep close to my heart. I will only grow in divine grace when I daily consecrate myself to God.

God wants me and He wants you. He isn't satisfied with only part, He wants it all. He wants our hopes and dreams, our frustrations and failures, our desires and our wills. When we can fully relinquish all of ourselves to Him, He is able to do exceedingly, abundantly more than we could ever expect in this life.

"Blessed is the one who perseveres under trial because, having stood the test, that person will receive the crown of life that the Lord has promised to those who love him." {James 1:12}

A mission ready marriage flourishes when God's role as Savior, Sanctifier, & Author of the sacred is recognized.

Questions for Reflection:

1. How do you define the words sanctify and sacred? Have either of these words held negative or intimidating connotations to you?

2. How has the sacrament of marriage, in particular, been a blessing of God's grace during your time as a military spouse? How do you see this from your vantage point? How might your spouse answer this about you?

3. Describe in your own words where you see yourself in the big picture of God's sanctifying work in your life? Where would you like to see yourself in the future? What do you think would be some good action steps to incorporate into your life to see this come to fruition? Are there physical things you could do? Or do you believe that these changes occur in the heart, mind, and attitude? Explain.

4. What are your personal feelings on the idea that God loves us, wants to give us the desires of our hearts, and see us happy? Can you find some Scriptural examples that support your viewpoints and theology of this?

5. Do you see your role as a military spouse as a form of personal ministry? If so, how? Do you think God can use His sacred blessings in big, transformative ways? How? And in your own life, where are you going to start looking? How do you plan to keep this sanctifying work of Christ Jesus as a reminder of the good life He's called you to?

Epilogue

Over the past few years I have needed a lot. I've needed assurance. I've needed peace. I have needed the roots of a strong, loving, and supportive family. I have needed the reminder that my home isn't so much about location or the type of house I live in, but rather all about the love found inside the four walls of any structure. Stuff is just stuff and we can't take it with us.

I have needed the reminder that God's provision isn't bound by time or space or geographical location. I have needed to learn the lesson that I am both strong and weak; both very capable and yet, very beautifully broken. Living in that tension is often right where God longs for me to be. I needed to walk through a deployment and a period of re-integration to recognize that I *can* do it all alone and yet, I *don't have to* do it at all by myself.

I have needed the experiences of the past few years to show me that any city or town can be great if you let it be; it's usually not the places but the people that make the greatest impact anyway. I needed to be schooled in the ways that I can be flexible when PCSing. God is in the details and yet, He longs for us to place our trust in Him more than those often illusive particulars of life.

I have needed to learn that re-inventing yourself is tiring and time consuming, but that my true identity is in Christ Jesus. I have learned that wise friends can teach us much about life and that if I desire to have a friend, I've first got to be a friend.

The greatest and most awe-inspiring lessons I have learned are that all of these matters I've needed resolution for in my life are *only* possible through my continual submission to Jesus Christ. The typical rites of passage in Army life are only able to be navigated successfully with God.

Only when I set aside self and die to my own sinful desires can I truly serve the Lord and allow Him to work in me. I then open myself up to His sanctifying process and am able to find gratitude for his sacred blessings.

It's somewhat comical to think back on these past few years when every single military experience was a novelty. It was all new! Every adversity felt big, dramatic, and emotional. From moving away from home, first assignments, and less than ideal duty stations, to first deployments and the pains of reintegration, God has had generous, copious amounts of material to use for my sanctification.

God has carefully crafted the events of the past few years to render something productive and conducive to that which He deems sacred. He has called our family, my husband, and

ME specifically to live my life with abandon and fully relinquished control to HIM.

That conclusion may seem simplistic or overly basic to many people. Your life may feel that way too. The mundane and enumerated daily tasks of being a military spouse can feel far from glamorous or enviable. But this is the one life the God of the universe has called you to live. He's called you to live it *for* Him and *in* Him and *through* Him.

I used to think that maybe God had given me this life as a military spouse as the thorn in my flesh, or my proverbial cross to bear this side of eternity. The longer I live, the more fallible and erroneous I believe that line of thinking to be. I now see this life as an honor and high calling. I know that when God gives me more than what I am capable of dealing with in my own strength, He will be with me even though it still feels heavy and burdensome. In fact, what He gives me is always less about showcasing my abilities and strengths and so much more about highlighting His goodness, faithfulness, and care.

God has handpicked me to be Ryan's wife and the mother to Thomas, Mae, and Kate. He has appointed a special ministry for me among my circle and sphere of influence. Some days that sphere is within the walls of my home as a loving, supportive wife and homeschooling mother of three. Other days that sphere extends to my neighborhood, to my chapel and women's ministry community, and to the bonds of friendship within our unit or in a workplace. *Every* day God has given me everything I need for this life! *Every* day God's divine gifts are mine to enjoy.

God has handpicked you and your spouse as a team to serve our great country. He has given *you* everything *you* need for this life. In order to flourish as a military spouse, are you willing and open to submitting your will to His? Would you allow God to prune away the ugly in favor of the new fruit? Can you spot all of his sacred offerings around you? God wants you mission ready! Are you ready for the assignment?

"His divine power has granted to us all things that pertain to life and godliness, through the knowledge of Him who called us to His own glory and excellence," {II Peter 1:3}

Notes

Introduction.

Link, Patrick E. and Palinkas, Lawrence A. "Long-Term Trajectories and Service Needs for Military Families." <u>Clinical Child and Family Psychology Review</u>. December 2013, Volume 16, Issue 4, pp 376-393.

Chapter 4.

Freeman, Emily P. <u>Grace For the Good Girl</u>. Revell. 2011.

Chapter 7.

Donne, John. "Meditation 17." <u>Devotions Upon Emergent Occasions</u>. 1624.

Chapter 11.

Hoffman, Beth. <u>Saving Cee Cee Honeycutt</u>. Penguin. 2010.

Chapter 12.

Lewis, Clive Staples. <u>Mere Christianity</u>. Public Domain. 1942-1944.

All passages of Scripture have been quoted from *The English Standard Version Bible*. New York: Oxford University Press, 2009. Print.

Acknowledgments

This book started as just an idea that maybe I have been able to learn something worth sharing during these past four years as a dependent. The lessons about how God can strengthen me, our marriage, and continue to make Ryan and me useful kingdom workers for the Lord in active duty military ministry are valuable to me. I've wondered if these truths might also be valuable to other military spouses who are looking for hope!

For the past eight years I have written hundreds of blog posts and thousands of words reflecting on what it means to live for the Lord as a wife, a mother, a woman, a teacher, and now a military spouse. As I began to realize the need for a resource in the hands of struggling military spouses, the organization and outline for this book came together. These are my stories about growing up and maturing as a military spouse and as a Believer. These are the stories of God's patience with and faithfulness toward me.

Every issue, every interaction, every tear and triumph has resulted from the relationships, experiences, and blessings I have made through our time in the Army.

I would like to thank:

Our former pastors and employers, Jim and Kathy Milligan. The ministry lessons they taught us and their unending support and encouragement of all of my dreams and Ryan's has been considerable.

Our endorsers and dear friends, Richard and Brenda Pace. You guys have made our transition to military ministry one of purpose and fulfillment. You have opened up your home and your hearts. Ryan and I are indebted to your example of love to the military community and your calling to mentor.

Our Fort Bliss First 1AD family, our Fort Gordon MI family, my PWOC sisters, our Redstone neighbors, Hardy Pointe neighbors, the wonderful sisterhood of chaplain spouses near and far; our First Tee family, and our friends and fellow supporters of various church and chapel communities. Thank you all for the depth of riches you add to our lives.

Our families, Mom, Dad, Ron, Becky, our siblings, in-laws, and extended family members. We miss living nearby but know God is in the details of our lives and locations. You have been our example, our strength, our support, and our safe place to land when we come home.

Our children, Thomas, Mae and Kate. Sometimes I can't believe how quickly these years are rolling by. You each amaze me with your resiliency, your constant joy no matter the circumstances and how (mostly) the three of you are just happily along for the ride. God knew what He was doing allowing Dad and I to have you spaced so closely together. He knew you'd need that blessed network of best buddies all within the walls of our home. Dad and I pray fervently that your exposure to our ministry would never sour you but rather, would spur you on to seek God, His plans and His promises for your lives.

My Ryan. We have had some tough patches figuring out this military calling over the past few years. There have been moments of absolute joy mixed with terrible heartache; there has been much good to come from our growth. Where there has been failure, forgiveness and grace has abounded more. There is no one else on this Earth that I would rather walk beside. You are my person; the one my soul loves! May the Lord continue to honor your efforts as a chaplain, multiply the ministry opportunities for each of us to serve Him, and let love abide in our hearts as we go forth mission ready.